OPPOSING
VIEWPOINTS®
SERIES

Understanding and Engaging Humanity

"Congress shall make no law . . . abridging the freedom of speech, or of the press."

First Amendment to the U.S. Constitution

The basic foundation of our democracy is the First Amendment guarantee of freedom of expression. The Opposing Viewpoints Series is dedicated to the concept of this basic freedom and the idea that it is more important to practice it than to enshrine it.

Understanding and Engaging Humanity

Brad McAdon, Mary E. Williams, Auriana Ojeda,
and William Dudley, Book Editors

GREENHAVEN PRESS
A part of Gale, Cengage Learning

Detroit • New York • San Francisco • New Haven, Conn • Waterville, Maine • London

Christine Nasso, *Publisher*
Elizabeth Des Chenes, *Managing Editor*

© 2010 Greenhaven Press, a part of Gale, Cengage Learning.

Gale and Greenhaven Press are registered trademarks used herein under license.

For more information, contact:
Greenhaven Press
27500 Drake Rd.
Farmington Hills, MI 48331-3535
Or you can visit our Internet site at gale.cengage.com

For product information and technology assistance, contact us at

Gale Customer Support, 1-800-877-4253
For permission to use material from this text or product, submit all requests online at www.cengage.com/permissions

Further permissions questions can be emailed to permissionrequest@cengage.com

Articles in Greenhaven Press anthologies are often edited for length to meet page requirements. In addition, original titles of these works are changed to clearly present the main thesis and to explicitly indicate the author's opinion. Every effort is made to ensure that Greenhaven Press accurately reflects the original intent of the authors. Every effort has been made to trace the owners of copyrighted material.

Cover images copyright joyfull, 2009; Yurlov Andrey, 2009; and Ximagination, 2009. All used under license from Shutterstock.com.

LIBRARY OF CONGRESS CATALOGING-IN-PUBLICATION DATA

Understanding and engaging humanity / Brad S. McAdon ... , book editors.
    p. cm. -- (Opposing viewpoints)
    Includes bibliographical references and index.
    ISBN 978-0-7377-4811-6 (pbk.)
    1. Humanism. 2. Civilization, Modern--Philosophy. I. McAdon, Brad S.
    B821.U53 2010
    128--dc22

                                                   2009033670

Printed in the United States of America
1 2 3 4 5   13 12 11 10 09
ED323

Contents

Chapter 3: What Motivates Moral Behavior?

Chapter 4: Should Limits Be Placed on Freedom of Expression?

Chapter 5: Addressing Social Inequalities

Why Consider Opposing Viewpoints?

> *"The only way in which a human being can make some approach to knowing the whole of a subject is by hearing what can be said about it by persons of every variety of opinion and studying all modes in which it can be looked at by every character of mind. No wise man ever acquired his wisdom in any mode but this."*
>
> John Stuart Mill

In our media-intensive culture it is not difficult to find differing opinions. Thousands of newspapers and magazines and dozens of radio and television talk shows resound with differing points of view. The difficulty lies in deciding which opinion to agree with and which "experts" seem the most credible. The more inundated we become with differing opinions and claims, the more essential it is to hone critical reading and thinking skills to evaluate these ideas. Opposing Viewpoints books address this problem directly by presenting stimulating debates that can be used to enhance and teach these skills. The varied opinions contained in each book examine many different aspects of a single issue. While examining these conveniently edited opposing views, readers can develop critical thinking skills such as the ability to compare and contrast authors' credibility, facts, argumentation styles, use of persuasive techniques, and other stylistic tools. In short, the Opposing Viewpoints Series is an ideal way to attain the higher-level thinking and reading skills so essential in a culture of diverse and contradictory opinions.

In addition to providing a tool for critical thinking, Opposing Viewpoints books challenge readers to question their own strongly held opinions and assumptions. Most people form their opinions on the basis of upbringing, peer pressure, and personal, cultural, or professional bias. By reading carefully balanced opposing views, readers must directly confront new ideas as well as the opinions of those with whom they disagree. This is not to simplistically argue that everyone who reads opposing views will—or should—change his or her opinion. Instead, the series enhances readers' understanding of their own views by encouraging confrontation with opposing ideas. Careful examination of others' views can lead to the readers' understanding of the logical inconsistencies in their own opinions, perspective on why they hold an opinion, and the consideration of the possibility that their opinion requires further evaluation.

Evaluating Other Opinions

To ensure that this type of examination occurs, Opposing Viewpoints books present all types of opinions. Prominent spokespeople on different sides of each issue as well as well-known professionals from many disciplines challenge the reader. An additional goal of the series is to provide a forum for other, less known, or even unpopular viewpoints. The opinion of an ordinary person who has had to make the decision to cut off life support from a terminally ill relative, for example, may be just as valuable and provide just as much insight as a medical ethicist's professional opinion. The editors have two additional purposes in including these less known views. One, the editors encourage readers to respect others' opinions—even when not enhanced by professional credibility. It is only by reading or listening to and objectively evaluating others' ideas that one can determine whether they are worthy of consideration. Two, the inclusion of such viewpoints encourages the important critical thinking skill of objectively evaluating an author's credentials and bias. This evaluation will illuminate an author's reasons for taking a particular stance on an issue and will aid in readers' evaluation of the author's ideas.

It is our hope that these books will give readers a deeper understanding of the issues debated and an appreciation of the complexity of even seemingly simple issues when good and honest people disagree. This awareness is particularly important in a democratic society such as ours in which people enter into public debate to determine the common good. Those with whom one disagrees should not be regarded as enemies but rather as people whose views deserve careful examination and may shed light on one's own.

Thomas Jefferson once said that "difference of opinion leads to inquiry, and inquiry to truth." Jefferson, a broadly educated man, argued that "if a nation expects to be ignorant and free . . . it expects what never was and never will be." As individuals and as a nation, it is imperative that we consider the opinions of others and examine them with skill and discernment. The Opposing Viewpoints Series is intended to help readers achieve this goal.

David L. Bender and Bruno Leone,
Founders

Introduction

> *"The evil that is in the world almost always comes of ignorance, and good intentions may do as much harm as malevolence if they lack understanding."*
>
> *Albert Camus*

One of the greatest challenges that instructors and administrators of composition programs face is selecting texts for their students to read. Of the many goals that administrators and faculty members seek to achieve in selecting texts—appropriate reading level and content for achieving the learning outcomes, user-friendliness, price, and more—one of the most important is settling upon material that will *engage* students and motivate them to read the material, learn from it, and even become active participants in the issues by writing thoughtfully about them. The selection of readings offered in this text accomplishes these goals by encouraging students to acquire a broader understanding of different worldviews and philosophies of life, by considering a variety of principles that guide our actions, and then by challenging readers to apply these principles to some of our most difficult social issues.

The first chapter invites readers to take a deeper look at their worldview. For example, M. Scott Peck, the author of the first selection, compares our view of reality to a map that we use to negotiate the terrain of life. In conscious and unconscious ways, Peck contends, we all construct our own individual maps, but we have a tendency to cling to the old, individual maps that served us in our childhood or youth. He encourages readers to confront the changes that life brings by continually revising their maps—a task that, he admits, demands courage and persistence. The other viewpoints in this chapter also draw attention to the fact that we are all encumbered with biases and preconceptions, and authors challenge readers to carefully reexamine their current beliefs and assumptions. In essence, the first chapter highlights the importance of having an open mind, the value of reason, and the necessity of curiosity—the first step toward wisdom and understanding.

After considering the need (or not) for developing a life philosophy in the first chapter, the second and third chapters continue the pursuit of wisdom by pondering questions such as the following: What do I really believe? How should I live my life? and What religious, scientific, or philosophical principles should guide my actions? The ideas presented in these chapters reflect the thinking of atheists and believers, skeptics and optimists, rationalists and mystics. For example, in Chapter 2, Richard Robinson expresses the opinion that this life is all there is and that humanity's finest accomplishment is to live with courage as it awaits its final extinction. Conversely, George E. Saint-Laurent argues that people practice religion because they are searching or reaching for some kind of meaning to their lives. Chapter 3 considers which religious, philosophical, or scientific principles should guide our moral behavior—our actions. Philip Yancey, former editor of *Christianity Today*, argues that separating moral behavior from God leads to the destruction of our social order, whereas Frank Zindler, former editor of *Atheist Magazine*, contends that ethical behavior has nothing to do with religious belief.

While Chapters 1 through 3 encourage readers to consider a variety of world views, to ask pointed questions about life's meaning, and to think about which principles guide their actions, Chapters 4 and 5 encourage readers to apply these important life principles to contemporary and complicated issues by pondering the question: How do I engage and respond to controversial civic and social issues? Chapter 4 considers the problems inherent in freedom of expression by examining issues that include whether hate speech should be regulated, whether desecrating the flag is an acceptable form of protest, and whether virtual child pornography should be banned. Chapter 5 offers opposing viewpoints that concern social inequalities by examining questions such as the following: Are African Americans oppressed in American society? Are affirmative action programs just? and Would reparations for slavery promote social justice?

Thus, this anthology provides its readers with opportunities to discuss some of the most basic, but challenging, questions of humankind, and then allows them to apply what is learned from these conversations to some of the most important and divisive social issues of our day. During the process of acquiring a broader understanding and applying that understanding to important issues, the essays here will also provide readers with many different kinds of claims, assertions, arguments, and other persuasive techniques that can be analyzed. An understanding of these persuasive techniques is essential to gain a better understanding of the essays themselves, for if readers cannot recognize the main points or claims of an argument, then much, if not all, of what the author is trying to communicate will be missed. So, join us, now, in this exciting journey from understanding, to analysis, to application—as much will be learned along the way.

CHAPTER 1

The Importance of Choosing a Life Philosophy

Chapter Preface

According to the Greek philosopher Socrates, one of the most noble accomplishments in life is for an individual to "know thyself." As the following chapter suggests, it is also one of the most challenging tasks because humans, like all creatures, have limitations. With our tendency to deceive ourselves, seek comfort, and avoid painful realities, the search for truth and self-awareness requires serious effort and courage. The authors in this chapter discuss what hinders and helps in one's quest for knowledge, personal growth, and commendable living.

In the first viewpoint, author and psychiatrist M. Scott Peck compares our understanding of the world to a map that we use to find our way through life. In other words, our view of reality guides us in our decision making processes, life choices, and search for meaning. The problem, according to Peck, is that our maps are often inaccurate. People may cling to small and limited maps—outmoded views of reality—that were effective during childhood, but not later in life. He maintains that we need to continually adjust our maps to accord with new truths that we encounter throughout our lives. Too often, however, we deceive ourselves because an honest examination of our lives and our problems can be painful. Peck believes that we must face this pain if we are dedicated to finding the truth.

In the second viewpoint, ancient philosopher Plato illustrates why humans resist adjusting their maps. In his famous allegorical dialogue, he reveals how people too quickly accept the world as it first appears to them. We often believe that the information we receive through our senses gives us reliable facts about our world, but the truth is that our senses provide a very limited view of reality. Truth, Plato suggests, lies beyond what we are ordinarily able to perceive. Consequently, we must use our reasoning abilities to find a fuller understanding of ourselves and our world.

In the third viewpoint, contemporary thinker Sam Keen explains that we need to discover the "myths" that can clarify our lives. Similar to Peck's concept of a life map, Keen defines myth as the dominating story lines that guide our culture, families, and individual lives. Keen believes that we must carefully examine the myths in which we are living because they likely contain destructive, yet creative elements. As we come to a more complete understanding of our own personal myth, we can make the adjustments that Peck and Plato challenge us to make in our lives.

The fourth viewpoint provides somewhat of a counterpoint to the previous three. Philosophy professor Charles Larmore warns that it is a mistake to believe that life is best lived in accord with a rational plan. In Larmore's opinion, the good things in life often come to us unexpectedly and have nothing to do with our own reasoning. While he does not believe that planning is pointless, he argues that the best choice of action lies somewhere between taking charge of our lives and letting life happen.

While Larmore questions the idea that the good life comes to us through planning and reasoning, he likely agrees with the other authors that we should avoid the temptation of accepting the world around us at simple face value. All of the authors in the following chapter invite us to seek the truth, a challenge that requires us to examine our most basic assumptions about ourselves and our world.

> *"Our view of reality is like a map with which to negotiate the terrain of life. If the map is true and accurate, we will generally know where we are."*

Choosing a Map for Life

M. Scott Peck

In the following viewpoint, M. Scott Peck compares the individual's view of reality to a map that is used to navigate through life. An accurate map provides solid guidance, but an incorrect map causes people to lose their way. Unfortunately, Peck argues, many people do not put enough effort into refining their views of reality. Their maps remain small and inaccurate, and they often hold onto narrow and outmoded ideas well into adulthood. Revising a map—that is, honestly facing the truth about reality and about one's life experiences—can be painful, but it is a necessary part of genuine human growth, Peck concludes. Peck, a psychiatrist and author, is best known for his 1978 book The Road Less Traveled, *from which this viewpoint is excerpted.*

M. Scott Peck, *The Road Less Traveled*. New York: Simon & Schuster, 1978. Copyright © 1978 by M. Scott Peck, MD. All rights reserved. Reprinted with the permission of Simon & Schuster, Inc.

As you read, consider the following questions:

1. Why do life maps need continual revision, in M. Scott Peck's opinion?

2. How does the author define transference?

3. In Peck's view, why do many people avoid a life of genuine self-examination?

Truth is reality. That which is false is unreal. The more clearly we see the reality of the world, the better equipped we are to deal with the world. The less clearly we see the reality of the world—the more our minds are befuddled by falsehood, misperceptions and illusions—the less able we will be to determine correct courses of action and make wise decisions.

Map of Life

Our view of reality is like a map with which to negotiate the terrain of life. If the map is true and accurate, we will generally know where we are, and if we have decided where we want to go, we will generally know how to get there. If the map is false and inaccurate, we generally will be lost.

While this is obvious, it is something that most people to a greater or lesser degree choose to ignore. They ignore it because our route to reality is not easy. First of all, we are not born with maps; we have to make them, and the making requires effort. The more effort we make to appreciate and perceive reality, the larger and more accurate our maps will be. But many do not want to make this effort. Some stop making it by the end of adolescence. Their maps are small and sketchy, their views of the world narrow and misleading. By the end of middle age most people have given up the effort. They feel certain that their maps are complete and their Weltanschauung [worldview, or assumptions] is correct (indeed, even sacrosanct), and they're no longer interested in new information. It is as if they are tired. Only a relative and fortunate few continue until the moment of death exploring the mystery of reality, ever enlarging and refining and redefining their understanding of the world and what is true.

Revising Life's Map

But the biggest problem of map-making is not that we have to start from scratch, but that if our maps are to be accurate we have to continually revise them. The world itself is constantly changing. Glaciers come, glaciers go. Cultures come, cultures go. There is too little technology, there is too much technology. Even more dramatically, the vantage point from which we view the world is constantly and quite rapidly changing. When we are children we are dependent, powerless. As adults we may be powerful. Yet in illness or an infirm old age we may become powerless and dependent again. When we have children to care for, the world looks different from when we have none; when we are raising infants, the world seems different from when we are raising adolescents. When we are poor, the world looks different from when we are rich. We are daily bombarded with new information as to the nature of reality. If we are to incorporate this information, we must continually revise our maps, and sometimes when enough new information has accumulated, we must make very major revisions. The process of making revisions, particularly major revisions, is painful, sometimes excruciatingly painful. And herein lies the major source of many of the ills of mankind.

What happens when one has striven long and hard to develop a working view of the world, a seemingly useful, workable map, and then is confronted with new information suggesting that that view is wrong and the map needs to be largely redrawn? The painful effort required seems frightening, almost overwhelming. What we do more often than not, and usually unconsciously, is to ignore the new information. Often this act of ignoring is much more than passive. We may denounce the new information as false, dangerous, heretical, the work of the devil. We may actually crusade against it, and even attempt to manipulate the world so as to make it conform to our view of reality. Rather than try to change the map, an individual may try to destroy the new reality. Sadly, such a person may expend much more energy ultimately in defending an outmoded view of the world than would have been required to revise and correct it in the first place.

This process of active clinging to an outmoded view of reality is the basis for much mental illness. Psychiatrists refer to it as transference. There are probably as many subtle variations of the definition of transference as there are psychiatrists. My own definition is: Transference is that set of ways of perceiving and responding to the world that is developed in childhood and is usually entirely appropriate to the childhood environment (indeed, often life-saving), but which is *inappropriately* transferred into the adult environment.

Examples of Transference

The ways in which transference manifests itself, while always pervasive and destructive, are often subtle. Yet the clearest examples must be unsubtle. One such example was a patient whose treatment failed by virtue of his transference. He was a brilliant, but unsuccessful computer technician in his early thirties, who came to see me because his wife had left him, taking their two children. He was not particularly unhappy to lose her, but he was devastated by the loss of his children, to whom he was deeply attached. It was in the hope of regaining them that he initiated psychotherapy, since his wife firmly stated she would never return to him unless he had psychiatric treatment. Her principal complaints about him were that he was continually and irrationally jealous of her, and yet at the same time aloof from her, cold, distant, uncommunicative and unaffectionate. She also complained of his frequent changes of employment. His life since adolescence had been markedly unstable. During adolescence he was involved in frequent minor altercations with the police, and had been jailed three times for intoxication, belligerence, "loitering," and "interfering with the duties of an officer." He dropped out of college, where he was studying electrical engineering, because, as he said, "My teachers were a bunch of hypocrites, hardly different from the police." Because of his brilliance and creativeness in the field of computer technology, his services were in high demand by the industry. But he had never been able to advance or keep a job for more than a year and a half occasionally being fired, more often quitting after disputes with his supervisors, whom he described as "liars and cheats, interested only in protecting their own ass." His most frequent expression was "You can't trust a goddam soul." He described his childhood as "normal" and his parents as "average." In the brief period of time he spent with me, however, he casually and unemotionally recounted numerous instances during childhood in which his parents had let him down. They promised him a bike for his birthday, but they forgot about it and gave him something else. Once they forgot his birthday entirely, but he saw nothing drastically wrong with this since "they were very busy." They would promise to do things with him on weekends, but then were usually "too busy." Numerous times they forgot to pick him up from meetings or parties because "they had a lot on their minds."

What happened to this man was that when he was a young child he suffered painful disappointment after painful disappointment through his parents' lack of caring. Gradually or suddenly—I don't know which—he came to the agonizing realization in mid-childhood that he could not trust his parents. Once he realized this, however, he began to feel better, and his life became more comfortable. He no longer expected things from his parents or got his hopes up when they made promises. When he stopped trusting his parents the frequency and severity of his disappointments diminished dramatically.

Such an adjustment, however, is the basis for future problems. To a child his or her parents are everything; they represent the world. The child does not have the perspective to see that other parents are different and frequently better. He assumes that the way his parents do things is the way that things are done. Consequently the realization—the "reality"—that this child came to was not "I can't trust my parents" but "I can't trust people." Not trusting people therefore became the map with which he entered adolescence and adulthood. With this map and with an abundant store of resentment resulting from his many disappointments, it was inevitable that he came into conflict with authority figures—police, teachers, employers. And these conflicts only served to reinforce his feeling that people who had anything to give him in the world couldn't be trusted. He had many opportunities to revise his map, but they were all passed up. For one thing, the only way he could learn that there were some people in the adult world he could trust would be to risk trusting them, and that would require a deviation from his map to begin with. For another, such relearning would require him to revise his view of his parents—to realize that they did not love him, that he did not have a normal childhood and that his parents were not average in their callousness to his needs. Such a realization would have been extremely painful. Finally, because his distrust of people was a realistic adjustment to the reality of his childhood, it was an adjustment that worked in terms of diminishing his pain and suffering. Since it is extremely difficult to give up an adjustment that once worked so well, he continued his course of distrust, unconsciously creating situations that served to reinforce it, alienating himself from everyone, making it impossible for himself to enjoy love, warmth, intimacy and affection. He could not even allow himself closeness with his wife; she, too, could not be trusted. The only people he could relate with intimately were his two children. They were the only ones over whom he had control, the only ones who had no authority over him, the only ones he could trust in the whole world.

When problems of transference are involved, as they usually are, psychotherapy is, among other things, a process of map-revising. Patients come to therapy because their maps are clearly not working. But how they may cling to them and fight the process every step of the way! Frequently their need to cling to their maps and fight against losing them is so great that therapy becomes impossible. . . .

Truth Can Overcome Transference

The problem of transference is not simply a problem between parents and children, husbands and wives, employers and employees, between friends, between groups, and even between nations. It is interesting to speculate, for instance, on the role that transference issues play in international affairs. Our national leaders are human beings who all had childhoods and childhood experiences that shaped them. What map was Hitler following, and where did it come from? What map were American leaders following in initiating, executing and maintaining the war in Vietnam? Clearly it was a map very different from that of the generation that succeeded theirs. In what ways did the national experience of the Depression years contribute to their map, and the experience of the fifties and sixties contribute to the map of the younger generation? If the national experience of the thirties and forties contributed to the behavior of American leaders in waging war in Vietnam, how appropriate was that experience to the realities of the sixties and seventies? How can we revise our maps more rapidly?

Truth or reality is avoided when it is painful. We can revise our maps only when we have the discipline to overcome that pain. To have such discipline, we must be totally dedicated to truth. That is to say that we must always hold truth, as best we can determine it, to be more important, more vital to our self-interest, than our comfort. Conversely, we must always consider our personal discomfort relatively unimportant and, indeed, even welcome it in the service of the search for truth. Mental health is an ongoing process of dedication to reality at all costs.

What does a life of total dedication to the truth mean? It means, first of all, a life of continuous and never-ending stringent self-examination. We know the world only through our relationship to it. Therefore, to know the world, we must not only examine it but we must simultaneously examine the examiner. . . .

Examination of the world without is never as personally painful as examination of the world within, and it is certainly because of the pain involved in a life of genuine self-examination that the majority steer away from it. Yet when one is dedicated to the truth this pain seems relatively unimportant—and less and less important (and therefore less and less painful) the farther one proceeds on the path of self-examination.

Accepting the Challenge

A life of total dedication to the truth also means a life of willingness to be personally challenged. The only way that we can be certain that our map of reality is valid is to expose it to the criticism and challenge of other map-makers. Otherwise we live in a closed system—within a bell jar, to use [poet] Sylvia Plath's analogy, rebreathing only our own fetid air, more and more subject to delusion. Yet, because of the pain inherent in the process of revising our map of reality, we mostly seek to avoid or ward off any challenges to its validity. To our children we say, "Don't talk back to me, I'm your parent." To our spouse we give the message, "Let's live and let live. If you criticize me, I'll be a bitch to live with, and you'll regret it." To their families and the world the elderly give the message, "I am old and fragile. If you challenge me I may die or at least

The Need to Examine Our Childhood Mind-Set

At age four or five ... [as] we begin to socialize, we internalize the values of family, peer group, religion, ethnic group, nationality, race, gender, and sexual orientation. The combination of [the following] two forces—the drive for happiness (in the form of security and survival, affection and esteem, and power and control) and overidentification with the particular group to which we belong—greatly complicates our emotional programs for happiness. In our younger days, this development is normal. As adults, activity arising from such motivation is childish. . . .

Our emotional programs are filtered through our temperamental biases. . . . If we have an aggressive temperament and like to dominate as many events and people as possible, that drive increases in proportion to the felt privations of that need that we suffered in early childhood. Without facing these early childhood [experiences] and trying to dismantle or moderate them through the exercise of reason ... they continue to exert enormous influence throughout life.

Thomas Keating, The Human Condition, *1999.*

you will bear upon your head the responsibility for making my last days on earth miserable." To our employees we communicate, "If you are bold enough to challenge me at all, you had best do so very circumspectly indeed or else you'll find yourself looking for another job."

The tendency to avoid challenge is so omnipresent in human beings that it can properly be considered a characteristic of human nature. But calling it natural does not mean it is essential or beneficial or unchangeable behavior. It is also natural to defecate in our pants and never brush our teeth. Yet we teach ourselves to do the unnatural until the unnatural becomes itself second nature. Indeed, all self-discipline might be defined as teaching ourselves to do the unnatural. . . .

For individuals and organizations to be open to challenge, it is necessary that their maps of reality be *truly* open for inspection. . . . It means a continuous and never-ending process of self-monitoring to assure that our communications— not only the words that we say but also the way we say them— invariably reflect as accurately as humanly possible the truth or reality as we know it.

Such honesty does not come painlessly. The reason people lie is to avoid the pain of challenge and its consequences. . . .

We lie, of course, not only to others but also to ourselves. The challenges to our adjustment—our maps—from our own consciences and our own realistic perceptions may be every bit as legitimate and painful as any challenge from the public . . . which is why most people opt for a life of very limited honesty and openness and relative closedness, hiding themselves and their maps from the world. It is easier that way. Yet the rewards of the difficult life of honesty and dedication to the truth are more than commensurate with the demands. By virtue of the fact that their maps are continually being challenged, open people are continually growing people.

| "[Imagine] human beings living in an underground den."

Living with Shadows in a Cave

Plato

Plato (c. 427–347 B.C.) was born into an aristocratic Athenian family and became the most well-known student of Socrates, whom he immortalized in his philosophical essays. Plato eventually founded the Academy, a school that endured for nearly one thousand years and that continues to influence the fields of ethics, philosophy, and theology. In the following allegorical dialogue, excerpted from The Republic, *Plato illustrates his belief that humans are separated from true reality by their subjective impressions of the world. People tend to accept their sensory perceptions as accurate representations of fact, Plato points out, but human senses only give a distorted reflection, or shadow, of reality. The unreliability of sensory experience means that people must carefully use reason as a tool to examine their beliefs.*

As you read, consider the following questions:

1. According to Plato, what happens first when a prisoner in a cave is released from his bonds?

Plato, *The Republic*, trans. Benjamin Jowett, 1894.

2. Once the prisoner has become accustomed to the light of the outside world, what feelings does he have about his fellow prison-mates, in Plato's opinion?

3. Once the released prisoner returns to the underground den, what do the other prisoners conclude about his experience, according to Plato?

And now, I said, let me show in a figure how far our nature is enlightened or unenlightened:—Behold! human beings living in an underground den, which has a mouth open towards the light and reaching all along the den; here they have been from their childhood, and have their legs and necks chained so that they cannot move, and can only see before them, being prevented by the chains from turning round their heads. Above and behind them a fire is blazing at a distance, and between the fire and the prisoners there is a raised way; and you will see, if you look, a low wall built along the way, like the screen which marionette players have in front of them, over which they show the puppets.

I see.

Strange Prisoners

And do you see, I said, men passing along the wall carrying all sorts of vessels, and statues and figures of animals made of wood and stone and various materials, which appear over the wall? Some of them are talking, others silent.

You have shown me a strange image, and they are strange prisoners.

Like ourselves, I replied; and they see only their own shadows, or the shadows of one another, which the fire throws on the opposite wall of the cave?

True, he said; how could they see anything but the shadows if they were never allowed to move their heads?

And of the objects which are being carried in like manner they would only see the shadows?

Yes, he said.

And if they were able to converse with one another, would they not suppose that they were naming what was actually before them?

Very true.

And suppose further that the prison had an echo which came from the other side, would they not be sure to fancy when one of the passers-by spoke that the voice which they heard came from the passing shadow?

No question, he replied.

To them, I said, the truth would be literally nothing but the shadows of the images.

That is certain.

Release of the Prisoners

And now look again, and see what will naturally follow if the prisoners are released and disabused of their error. At first, when any of them is liberated and compelled suddenly to stand up and turn his neck round and walk and look towards the light, he will suffer sharp pains; the glare will distress him, and he will be unable to see the realities of which in his former state he had seen the shadows; and then conceive some one saying to him, that what he saw before was an illusion, but that now, when he is approaching nearer to being and his eye is turned towards more real existence, he has a clearer vision—what will be his reply? And you may further imagine that his instructor is pointing to the objects as they pass and requiring him to name them—will he not be perplexed? Will he not fancy that the shadows which he formerly saw are truer than the objects which are now shown to him?

Far truer.

And if he is compelled to look straight at the light, will he not have a pain in his eyes which will make him turn away to take refuge in the objects of vision which he can see, and which he will conceive to be in reality clearer than the things which are now being shown to him?

True, he said.

Leaving the Cave

And suppose once more, that he is reluctantly dragged up a steep and rugged ascent, and held fast until he is forced into the presence of the sun himself, is he not likely to be pained and irritated? When he approaches the light his eyes will be dazzled, and he will not be able to see anything at all of what are now called realities.

Not all in a moment, he said.

He will require to grow accustomed to the sight of the upper world. And first he will see the shadows best, next the reflections of men and other objects in the water, and then the objects themselves; then he will gaze upon the light of the moon and the stars and the spangled heaven; and he will see the sky and the stars by night better than the sun or the light of the sun by day?

Certainly.

Last of all he will be able to see the sun, and not mere reflections of him in the water, but he will see him in his own proper place, and not in another; and he will contemplate him as he is.

Certainly.

He will then proceed to argue that this is he who gives the season and the years, and is the guardian of all that is in the visible world, and in a certain way the cause of all things which he and his fellows have been accustomed to behold?

Clearly, he said, he would first see the sun and then reason about him.

And when he remembered his old habitation, and the wisdom of the den and his fellow prisoners, do you not suppose that he would felicitate himself on the change, and pity them?

Certainly, he would.

And if they were in the habit of conferring honors among themselves on those who were quickest to observe the passing shadows and to remark which of them went before, and which followed after, and which were together; and who were therefore best able to draw conclusions as to the future, do you think that he would care for such honors and glories, or envy the possessors of them? Would he not say with Homer, "Better to be the poor servant of a poor master," and to endure anything, rather than think as they do and live after their manner?

Yes, he said, I think that he would rather suffer anything than entertain these false notions and live in this miserable manner.

Returning to the Cave

Imagine once more, I said, such a one coming suddenly out of the sun to be replaced in his old situation; would he not be certain to have his eyes full of darkness?

To be sure, he said.

And if there were a contest, and he had to compete in measuring the shadows with the prisoners who had never moved out of the den, while his sight was still weak, and before his eyes had become steady (and the time which would be needed to acquire this new habit of sight might be very considerable), would he not be ridiculous? Men would say of him that up he went and down he came without his eyes; and that it was better not even to think of ascending; and if any one tried to loose another and lead him up to the light, let them only catch the offender, and they would put him to death.

No question, he said.

Conclusion

This entire allegory, I said, you may now append, dear Glaucon, to the previous argument; the prison house is the world of sight, the light of the fire is the sun, and you will not mis-apprehend me if you interpret the journey upwards to be the ascent of the soul into the intellectual world according to my poor belief, which, at your desire, I have expressed—whether rightly or wrongly God knows. But, whether true or false, my opinion is that in the world of knowledge the idea of good appears last of all, and is seen only with an effort; and, when seen, is also inferred to be the universal author of all things beautiful and right, parent of light and of the Lord of light in this visible world, and the immediate source of reason and truth in the intellectual; and that this is the power upon which he who would act rationally either in public or private life must have his eye fixed.

> "We gain personal authority and power in the measure that we . . . discover and create a personal myth that illuminates and informs us."

Discovering Our Personal Myth

Sam Keen

Sam Keen is a former professor of philosophy and religion and a former contributing editor of Psychology Today. *He is currently a lecturer, consultant, and author who has written more than a dozen books on myth, spirituality, and self-improvement. The following viewpoint is taken from his preface to* Your Mythic Journey, *a book he co-authored with educator and writer Anne Valley-Fox. In this excerpt, Keen discusses the significance of myth, which he defines as the combination of customs, traditions, stories, and philosophies that form each individual's understanding of life. Keen argues that it is important for people to discover the myth that has shaped their lives, so they can consciously update it, retaining what is beneficial, rejecting what is harmful, and adding new ideas gleaned from personal experience.*

As you read, consider the following questions:

1. How is myth commonly defined, according to Sam Keen, and how does this popular definition differ from the author's definition?

2. In what way can the inherent conservatism of myth be destructive, in the author's opinion?

3. According to Keen, how can individuals gain personal authority and power?

It seems that Americans are finally taking seriously what Carl Jung, the Swiss psychologist, said is the most important question we can ask ourselves: "What myth are we living?"...

What Is a Myth?

What is a myth? Few words have been subject to as much abuse and been as ill-defined as *myth*. Journalists usually use it to mean a "lie," "fabrication," "illusion," "mistake," or something similar. It is the opposite of what is supposedly a "fact," of what is "objectively" the case, and of what is "reality." In this usage myth is at best a silly story and at worst a cynical untruth. Theologians and propagandists often use myth as a way of characterizing religious beliefs and ideologies other than their own.

Such trivialization of the notion of myth reflects false certainties of dogmatic minds, an ignorance of the mythic assumptions that underlie the commonly accepted view of "reality," and a refusal to consider how much our individual and communal lives are shaped by dramatic scenarios and "historical" narratives that are replete with accounts of the struggle between good and evil empires: our godly heroes versus the demonic enemy.

In a strict sense *myth* refers to "an intricate set of interlocking stories, rituals, rites, and customs that inform and give the pivotal sense of meaning and direction to a person, family, community, or culture." A living myth, like an iceberg, is 10 percent visible and 90 percent beneath the surface of consciousness. While it involves a conscious celebration of certain values, which are always personified in a pantheon of heroes (from the wily Ulysses to the managing [former CEO of Chrysler Corporation] Lee Iacocca) and villains (from the betraying Judas to the barbarous [president of Libya] Moammar Kadafi), it also includes the unspoken consensus, the habitual way of seeing things, the unquestioned assumptions, the automatic stance. It is differing cultural myths that make cows sacred objects for Hindus and hamburger meals for Methodists, or turn dogs into pets for Americans and roasted delicacies for the Chinese.

At least 51 percent of the people in a society are not self-consciously aware of the myth that informs their existence. Cultural consensus is created by an unconscious conspiracy to consider the myth "the truth," "the way things *really* are." In other words, a majority is made up of literalists, men and women who are not critical or reflective about the guiding "truths"—myths—of their own group. To a tourist in a strange land, an anthropologist studying a tribe, or a psychologist observing a patient, the myth is obvious. But to the person who lives within the mythic horizon, it is nearly invisible.

For instance, most Americans would consider potlatch feasts, in which Northwest Indian tribes systematically destroy their wealth, to be irrational and mythic but would consider the habit of browsing in malls and buying expensive things we do not need (conspicuous consumption) to be a perfectly reasonable way to spend a Saturday afternoon. To most Americans the Moslem notion of *jihad*—holy war—is a dangerous myth. But our struggle against "atheistic communism" is a righteous duty. Ask a born-again Christian about the myth of the atonement, and you will be told it is no myth at all but a revealed truth. Ask a true believer of Marxism about the myth of the withering away of the state, and you will get a long explanation about the "scientific" laws of the dialectic of history.

I suggest two analogies that may help to counteract the popular trivialized notion of myth. The dominant myth that informs a person or a culture is like the "information" contained in DNA or the program in the systems disk of a computer. Myth is the software, the cultural DNA, the unconscious information, the metaprogram that governs the way we see "reality" and the way we behave.

Myths Can Be Creative or Destructive

The organizing myth of any culture functions in ways that may be either creative or destructive, healthful or pathological. By providing a world picture and a set of stories that explain why things are as they are, it creates consensus, sanctifies the social order, and gives the individual an authorized map of the path of life. A myth creates the plotline that organizes the diverse experiences of a person or a community into a single story.

But in the same measure that myth gives us security and identity, it also creates selective blindness, narrowness, and rigidity because it is intrinsically conservative. It encourages us to follow the faith of our fathers, to hold to the time-honored truths, to imitate the way of the heroes, to repeat the formulas and rituals in exactly the same way they were done in the good old days. As long as no radical change is necessary for survival, the status quo remains sacred, the myth and ritual are unquestioned, and the patterns of life, like the seasons of the year, repeat themselves. But when crisis comes—a natural catastrophe, a military defeat, the introduction of a new technology—the mythic mind is at a loss to deal with novelty. As [educator] Marshall McLuhan said, it tries to "walk into the future looking through a rearview mirror."

The Functions of Myth

Michael Toms: Myth . . . informs us about the stage of life we're in. Isn't that so?

Joseph Campbell: Yes. Actually, that's one of the main functions of myth. It's what I call the pedagogical: to carry a person through the inevitable stages of a lifetime. And these are the same today as they were in the Paleolithic caves: as a youngster you're dependent on parents to teach you what life is, and what your relationship to other people has to be, and so forth; then you give up that dependence to become a self-responsible authority; and, finally, comes the stage of yielding: you realize that the world is in other hands. And the myth tells you what the values are in those stages in terms of the possibilities of your particular society.

Michael Toms,
An Open Life: Joseph Campbell in
Conversation with Michael Toms, *1989.*

Families Have Myths

Every family, like a miniculture, also has an elaborate system of stories and rituals that differentiate it from other families. The Murphys, being Irish, understand full well that Uncle Paddy is a bit of a rogue and drinks a tad too much. The Cohens, being Jewish, are haunted each year at Passover when they remember the family that perished in the Holocaust. The Keens, being Calvinists, are predestined to be slightly more righteous and right than others, even when they are wrong. And within the family each member's place is defined by a series of stories. Obedient to the family script, Jane, "who always was very motherly even as a little girl," married young and had children immediately, while Pat, "who was a wild one and not cut out for marriage," sowed oat after oat before finding fertile ground.

Family myths, like those of the Kennedy clan, may give us an impulse to strive for excellence and a sense of pride that helps us endure hardship and tragedy. Or they may, like the myths of alcoholic or abusive families, pass a burden of guilt, shame, and failure from generation to generation as abused children, in turn, become abusive parents, ad nauseam. The sins, virtues, and myths of the fathers are passed on to the children of future generations.

Every Individual Has a Personal Myth

Finally, the entire legacy and burden of cultural and family myth comes to rest on the individual. Each person is a repository of stories. To the degree that any one of us reaches toward autonomy, we must begin a process of sorting through the trash and treasures we have been given, keeping some and rejecting others. We gain the full dignity and power of our persons only when we create a narrative account of our lives, dramatize our existence, and forge a coherent personal myth that combines elements of our cultural myth and family myth with unique stories that come from our experience. As my friend David Steere once pointed out to me, the common root of "authority" and "authorship" tells us a great deal about power. Whoever authors your story authorizes your actions. We gain personal authority and power in the measure that we question the myth that is upheld by "the authorities" and discover and create a personal myth that illuminates and informs us.

What [philosopher] George Santayana said about cultures is equally true for individuals: "Those who do not remember history are condemned to repeat it." If we do not make the effort to become conscious of our personal myths gradually, we become dominated by what psychologists have variously called repetition compulsion, autonomous complexes, engrams, routines, scripts, games. One fruitful way to think of neurosis is to consider it a tape loop, an oft-told story that we repeat in our inner dialogues with ourselves and with others. "Well, I'm just not the kind of person who can . . ." "I never could . . ." "I wouldn't think of . . ." While personal myths give us a sense of identity, continuity and security, they become constricting and boring if they are not revised from time to time. To remain vibrant throughout a lifetime we must always be inventing ourselves, weaving new themes into our life narratives, remembering our past, re-visioning our future, reauthorizing the myth by which we live.

| "The idea that life should be the object of a plan is false to the human condition."

Challenging the Idea of a Life Plan

Charles Larmore

In the following viewpoint, Charles Larmore challenges the notion that people will live a good life by following the precepts of a rational plan. This idea of controlling one's life through reason and planning has been espoused by ancient and modern philosophers, but human experience reveals that happiness is often the result of unanticipated events, Larmore points out. Moreover, the good that people pursue often falls short of the good that happens to them unexpectedly. While there is nothing wrong with organizing and shaping one's life, people should also recognize that unforeseen experiences will challenge their plans and enhance their lives in unpredictable ways. Larmore is a professor of political science and philosophy at the University of Chicago.

Charles Larmore, "The Idea of a Life Plan," *Social Philosophy & Policy*, vol. 16, Winter 1999, pp. 96–98. Cambridge University Press, 1999. Reprinted with the permission of Cambridge University Press.

As you read, consider the following questions:

1. According to Charles Larmore, what was one of the main themes of Marcel Proust's *À la recherche du temps perdu* [*Remembrance of Things Past*]?

2. Between what two extremes does the good life lie, in the author's opinion?

3. How does being passive contribute to living a good life, in Larmore's view?

When philosophers undertake to say what it is that makes life worth living, they generally display a procrustean habit of thought which the practice of philosophy itself does much to encourage. As a result, they arrive at an image of the human good that is far more controversial than they suspect. The canonical view among philosophers ancient and modern has been, in essence, that the life lived well is the life lived in accord with a rational plan. To me this conception of the human good seems manifestly wrong. The idea that life should be the object of a plan is false to the human condition. It misses the important truth which [French writer Marcel] Proust, by contrast, discerned and made into one of the organizing themes of his great meditation on disappointment and revelation *À la recherche du temps perdu* [*Remembrance of Things Past*]. The happiness that life affords is less often the good we have reason to pursue than the good that befalls us unexpectedly.

The mistake to which I refer has molded the way that philosophy on the whole has dealt with the most fundamental question we ask ourselves, the question of how we are to live our lives. I do not believe that there has been anything inevitable about this development, anything inherent in the philosophical enterprise that has led to the mistaken ideal of a life plan. It is not the very nature of philosophy which is to blame, for philosophy really has no essence beyond the goal of com-

What Life Gives Us

In exchange for what our imagination leads us to expect and which we vainly give ourselves so much trouble to try to discover, life gives us something which we were very far from imagining.

Marcel Proust, Albertine Disparue, *1925.*

prehensive understanding, and that may mean a great many things. But I am convinced that philosophers have by and large proceeded on the wrong track in dealing with this question, and that their error is more than accidental, stemming as it does from what has been one of their abiding preoccupations.

Do We Really Lead Our Lives?

Before explaining this point further, I should indicate what precisely I believe is wrong in the idea of a life plan. The mistake lies at its very core, in the basic attitude toward life to which it gives expression. That attitude is the view that a life is something we are to lead and not something we should allow to happen to us. We flourish as human beings, it supposes, only if we shape our lives ourselves, instead of leaving them to be the hostages of circumstance and whim. If this is our outlook, then we should obviously seek to live in accord with some unified conception of our overall purposes and of the ways to achieve them. In other words, we should devise for ourselves some "plan of life" at least in its broad strokes, if not fine-tuned in its smallest details. To the extent that we work out our plan in a rational way, giving due weight to our beliefs about what is valuable, our knowledge of our own abilities, and our grasp of the possibilities the world provides, we will have determined the character of our good and the way to achieve it. Success is not guaranteed, of course; but we will have done the best we could.

This conception of life seems perhaps so sensible that we may wonder what could be amiss. The rub, I am inclined to say, is that it is too sensible. But no doubt the better and more straightforward way to put the objection is by observing that this frame of mind embodies too great a timidity in the face of the power that experience has to change our sense of what makes life worth living. Its guiding assumption is that we should take charge of our lives, bringing them under our rule as best we can. And yet we go wrong in making so much of a contrast between leading a life and letting life happen to us. The good lies between these two extremes. It belongs to a life that is not just led but met with as well, a life that is both self-directed and shaped from without. We miss an important aspect of what gives our lives meaning, when we suppose that we live well by living in accord with an all-embracing plan of our own devising. The happy life spans, not just the good we plan for, but also the unlooked-for good which befalls us.

The basis of my opposition to the idea of a life plan is not, I should observe, the age-old perception that the best-laid schemes of mice and men go oft awry. Our plans, when we put them into practice, certainly risk defeat at the hands of reality. And disappointment may seem inescapable when so complicated a matter as life itself is made the object of a plan. Many people have raised this sort of difficulty, none perhaps so movingly as Samuel Johnson in *Rasselas* (published in 1759). In this novel, the young prince Rasselas, cloyed by his pampered existence in the Happy Valley, escapes to make his own way in the world. His faith is that with experience will come the ability to make, as he says, the proper "choice of life." But Imlac, his tutor, tries to disabuse him of this hope. Our grasp of how the world is put together is too unreliable

Let Beauty Surprise You

Beauty is a free spirit and will not be trapped within the grid of intentionality. . . .

The wonder of the beautiful is its ability to surprise us. With swift, sheer grace, it is like a divine breath that blows the heart open. Immune to our strategies, it can take us when we least expect it. Because our present habit of mind is governed by the calculus of consumerism and busyness, we are less and less frequently available to the exuberance of beauty. Indeed, we have brought calculation to such a level that it now seems unsophisticated to admit surprise.

John O'Donohue, Beauty: The Invisible Embrace, *2004.*

for any such choice to stand a real chance of success. "The causes of good and evil," Imlac insists,

> are so various and uncertain, so often entangled with each other, so diversified by various relations, and so much subject to accidents which cannot be foreseen that he who would fix his condition upon incontestable reasons of preference, must live and die inquiring and deliberating. . . . Very few live by choice. Every man is placed in his present condition by causes which acted without his foresight, and with which he did not always willingly cooperate.

There is considerable wisdom in these observations, but they do not really suffice to undermine the idea of a life plan. Snarled and unpredictable though the ways of the world may be, we can set our sights on ends whose achievement seems minimally imperiled by chance or misfortune. To choose our purposes with an eye to lessening the likelihood of frustration has been, after all, the almost universal advice of the philosophical tradition, the grounds on which it has often elevated, for example, the life of virtue above the pursuit of more fickle goods such as honor or wealth. Probably no way of life can escape altogether the play of luck. But the fragility of whatever good we may achieve is not the point I am concerned to make.

My protest against the idea of a life plan is of a different and more fundamental kind. It arises not from the precariousness of our plans, but rather from the drawbacks of planning. A significant dimension of the human good escapes us if we believe that our attitude toward life must be at the bottom, one of foresight and control, as the idea of a life plan entails.

On the contrary, we live well when we are not simply active, but passive too. There is an openness to life's surprises which we do well to maintain. For the unexpected can turn out to be, not just the mishap that defeats our plans, but also the revelation that discloses new vistas of meaning, new forms of happiness and understanding which we least suspected or never imagined and which may change our lives and who we are in the deepest way. Sometimes we then learn that we have been mistaken in the things we have hitherto had reason to value. Other times we find simply that we must add a new element to our notion of our good (though the addition often ends up affecting the complexion of our other commitments as well). . . .

Life Is Unruly

Life is too unruly to be the object of a plan, and again not simply because our schemes may founder when applied. Obviously, we often fail to achieve the good we pursue. But more important and certainly more neglected by philosophy is the happy fact that the good we pursue, the good we have reason to pursue, is bound to fall short of the good that life has yet to reveal. From this insight we should not infer that the nature of the good life is a question not worth trying to answer since every answer will prove inadequate. It is natural to think about what elements go into making up our good, and my remarks have not been meant to deny that each of us lives, or ought to live, with an idea in mind of the good life. The target of my criticism has been the view that any such idea must be of a life we have taken charge of and brought under the rule of our own purposes. The good life is not, I have argued, the life lived in accord with a rational plan. It is the life lived with a sense of our dual nature as active and passive beings, bent on achieving the goals we espouse, but also liable to be surprised by forms of good we never anticipated. A life lived in the light of this more complex ideal can accommodate, it can even welcome, the way in which an unexpected good may challenge our existing projects. We will not thereby avoid being surprised (nor should we want to), but we will know enough not to be surprised at being surprised.

Nothing I have said should suggest, either, that planning is wrong or pointless. Prudence is an undeniable virtue, and not solely in the handling of the little things of life. We cannot hope to live well if we do not direct ourselves toward achieving goals which have a ramifying significance, which organize our various activities and give our lives meaning. But we err if we suppose that prudence is the supreme virtue and that the good life is one which unfolds in accord with a rational plan.

OPPOSING
VIEWPOINTS®
SERIES

CHAPTER 2

What Reveals Life's Ultimate Meaning?

Chapter Preface

Philosophers, sages, theologians, and scientists have responded to the question "Why is there something rather than nothing?" in various ways. For example, some existentialist philosophers contend that such a question is unanswerable, and that one should ask instead "What should we do with this 'something' in which we live?" For them, life's meaning rests in the freedom to choose—a freedom that entails commitment and responsibility, but avoids an unquestioning reliance on commonly accepted beliefs. Many religious believers, on the other hand, maintain that human existence results from the creative act of a supreme being who cannot be perceived through our senses or reasoning. They envision life as a divinely conceived path that leads humans from alienation and self-centeredness to some form of salvation or enlightenment. Scientists, however, seek to discover life's mysteries through observable data, precise experimentation, and theoretical speculation. While most scientists agree that science cannot answer the question of *why* the universe exists, it can help us see *how* the universe works and what role humanity plays in it. With the information gleaned from science, humans can shape their future, creating meaning and purpose as they learn and evolve.

The authors in the following chapter present different answers to the question of what reveals life's meaning. Twentieth-century philosopher Richard Robinson argues that no ultimate "secret" of the universe and no supreme being exist. He contends, however, that humans can find meaning in promoting self-chosen virtues and in loving one another as they face their coming extinction. Comparative religion scholar George E. Saint-Laurent discusses how religious believers pursue meaning through communion with the sacred, a mystery that at once permeates and transcends human senses and intellect.

Physics instructor Wayne Anderson maintains that the discoveries of science offer a solid intellectual basis for understanding how humans fit into natural and cosmic processes. He believes that science will eventually play a role in usurping religion's reliance on a supreme being for meaning. On the other hand, science writer and editor Sharon Begley contends that both faith and science provide genuine insights into the mysteries of the universe and the meaning of human life. She suggests that while science and religion respond to the question of meaning in different ways, each can heal the excesses of the other: Science can cleanse religion of its superstition, and religion can rid science of its arrogance.

While these authors may disagree on where to find life's meaning, they all share a concern for human welfare and ponder what role humanity plays in the cosmos. Their musings on choice, science, faith, and reason offer fascinating insights relevant to the construction of a life philosophy.

> *"There is no possibility of 'making sense of the Universe,' if that means discovering one truth about it which explains everything else about it and also explains itself."*

Ultimate Meaning Does Not Exist

Richard Robinson

Richard Robinson (1902–1996) taught philosophy at Cornell University in Ithaca, New York, and at Oxford University in England. In the following viewpoint, excerpted from his book An Atheist's Values, *Robinson argues that no single truth can explain the existence of the universe and no God will rescue humanity from disasters and death. Given these circumstances, humans should accept their predicament and face their future with courage, cheerfulness, and dignity. Since humans are alone in the universe, Robinson contends, their most noble and life-affirming choice is to pursue goodness, truth, and human solidarity.*

As you read, consider the following questions:

1. Why are humans permanently insecure, in Richard Robinson's opinion?

Richard Robinson, *An Atheist's Values.* Oxford, UK: Blackwell, 1975. Copyright © 1975 by Basil Blackwell Ltd. Reproduced by permission of Blackwell Publishers.

2. In the author's view, why is atheism more noble than theism?

3. According to Robinson, why do humans need to create new ceremonies?

The human situation is this. Each one of us dies. He ceases to pulse or breathe or move or think. He decays and loses his identity. His mind or soul or spirit ends with the ending of his body, because it is entirely dependent on his body.

The human species too will die one day, like all species of life. One day there will be no more men. This is not quite so probable as that each individual man will die; but it is overwhelmingly probable all the same. It seems very unlikely that we could keep the race going forever by hopping from planet to planet as each in turn cooled down. Only in times of extraordinary prosperity like the present could we ever travel to another planet at all.

We are permanently insecure. We are permanently in danger of loss, damage, misery, and death.

Our insecurity is due partly to our ignorance. There is a vast amount that we do not know, and some of it is very relevant to our survival and happiness. It is not just one important thing that we can ascertain and live securely ever after. That one important thing would then deserve to be called 'the secret of the universe'. But there is no one secret of the universe. On the contrary, there are inexhaustibly many things about the universe that we need to know but do not know. There is no possibility of 'making sense of the universe', if that means discovering one truth about it which explains everything else about it and also explains itself. Our ignorance grows progressively less, at least during periods of enormous prosperity like the present time; but it cannot disappear, and must always leave us liable to unforeseen disasters.

The main cause of our insecurity is the limitedness of our power. What happens to us depends largely on forces we cannot always control. This will remain so throughout the life of our species, although our power will probably greatly increase.

There Is No God

There is no God to make up for the limitations of our power, to rescue us whenever the forces affecting us get beyond our control, or provide us hereafter with an incorruptible haven of absolute security. We have no superhuman father who is perfectly competent and benevolent as we perhaps once supposed our actual father to be.

What attitude ought we to take up, in view of this situation? It would be senseless to be rebellious, since there is no God to rebel against. It would be wrong to let disappointment or terror or apathy or folly overcome us. It would be wrong to be sad or sarcastic or cynical or indignant....

Cheerfulness is part of courage, and courage is an essential part of the right attitude. Let us not tell ourselves a comforting tale of a father in heaven because we are afraid to be alone, but bravely and cheerfully face whatever appears to be the truth.

Theism Versus Atheism

The theist sometimes rebukes the pleasure-seeker by saying: *We were not put here to enjoy ourselves: Man has a sterner and nobler purpose than that.* The atheist's conception of man is, however, still sterner and nobler than that of the theist. According to the theist we were put here by an all-powerful and all-benevolent God who will give us eternal victory and happiness if we only obey him. According to the atheist our situation is far sterner than that. There is no one to look after us but ourselves, and we shall certainly be defeated.

As our situation is far sterner than the theist dares to think, so our possible attitude towards it is far nobler than he conceives. When we contemplate the friendless position of man in the universe, as it is right sometimes to do, our attitude should be the tragic poet's affirmation of man's ideals of behaviour. Our dignity, and our finest occupation, is to assert and maintain our own self-chosen goods as long as we can, those great goods of beauty and truth and virtue. And among the virtues it is proper to mention in this connection above all the virtues of courage and love. There is no person in this universe to love us except ourselves; therefore let us love one another. The human race is alone; but individual men need not be alone, because we have each other. We are brothers without a father; let us all the more for that behave brotherly to each other. The finest achievement for humanity is to recognize our predicament, including our insecurity and our coming extinction, and to maintain our cheerfulness and love and decency in spite of it. We have good things to contemplate and high things to do. Let us do them.

We need to create and spread symbols and procedures that will confirm our intentions without involving us in intellectual dishonesty. This need is urgent today. For we have as yet no strong ceremonies to confirm our resolves except religious ceremonies, and most of us cannot join in religious ceremonies with a good conscience. When the *Titanic* went down, people sang 'nearer, my God, to thee'. When the Gloucesters were in prison in North Korea they strengthened themselves with religious ceremonies. At present we know no other way to strengthen ourselves in our most testing and tragic times. Yet this way has become dishonest. That is why it is urgent for us to create new ceremonies, through which to find strength without falsehood in these terrible situations. It is not enough to formulate honest and high ideals. We must also create the ceremonies and the atmosphere that will hold them before us at all times. I have no conception how to do this; but I believe it will be done if we try.

> *"People practice religion in the more or less conscious quest for human significance."*

Religion Pursues Life's Meaning

George E. Saint-Laurent

The major world religions pursue answers to questions about humanity's origins, purpose, and future, writes George E. Saint-Laurent in the following viewpoint. Religion also prescribes a way, or path, that guides behavior and leads to transformation, salvation, or enlightenment. Judaism, Christianity, Islam, Hinduism, and Buddhism all profess that ultimate meaning resides in a sacred dimension or absolute reality that transcends human senses or intellect, the author explains. Each of these religions also teaches that human transformation entails the rejection of a self-centered life and an embracing of the divine will. Saint-Laurent is an emeritus professor of comparative religion and spirituality at California State University in Fullerton.

As you read, consider the following questions:

1. What are "life's great questions," according to Saint-Laurent?

George E. Saint-Laurent, *Spirituality and World Religions: A Comparative Introduction*, Mountain View, CA: Mayfield Publishing Company, 2000, pp. 22–27. Copyright © 2000 Mayfield Publishing. Reproduced by permission of McGraw-Hill, Inc.

2. According to the author, what do Jews, Christians, and Muslims see as humanity's central problem? How do Hindus and Buddhists define the human predicament?

3. Why is it that theological language can provide only an indirect description of the sacred, in Saint-Laurent's view?

Religion is a *pursuit*, and religious persons must be prepared to make a sustained effort throughout their life. Religion can be an idyllic search for absolute truth, love, and beauty, but it can also demand a rigorous program of performance. An authentic faith commitment usually engenders a practical way of life and can even create a whole culture, as in the case of medieval Christendom. That is why Moses, the Buddha, Jesus, and Muhammad required that their disciples not only hope in the future, but also apply themselves to virtuous conduct here and now. These men were teachers of uncommon vision, but they were also men of action who marshaled all their physical energy and inner resources toward their life's mission.

People practice religion in the more or less conscious quest for human significance. They often feel that they would be troubled, incomplete, and restless without their religion. Religious men and women seek satisfying answers to life's great questions: From where have I come, what does it mean to be a human being, why am I here, and what will happen to me after death? To the extent that practitioners faithfully adhere to the teachings of their tradition, they discover a new meaning in life. Of course, authentic faith should bear fruit in practice. Religious people have a framework of meditation and/or rituals of prayerful worship to purify their intentions and ethical criteria to discipline their activity. Devotees learn to interpret their daily experiences from a perspective of inspiring vision and lasting values. As their spirituality deepens and matures, they often feel a new conviction of purpose and mission, perhaps even a sense of vocation and election "from above."

The Pursuit of Transformation

Religion is the pursuit of *transformation*. Religious people want to integrate harmoniously all the levels of their humanity. They long for liberation from whatever traps and binds them. They seek healing from every scar of past brokenness, elevation to a new dimension of consciousness, and transfiguration according to their new ideal of complete personhood.

Jews, Christians, Muslims, Hindus, and Buddhists all teach a source of meaning not of this world: a confirmation in peace (Hebrew *shalom*, Greek *eirene*, Arabic *salam*, Sanskrit *shanti*, and Pali *santi*). They also agree that we initially find ourselves in a dehumanizing predicament of disease. Human life, indeed, abounds with difficulties of every description, but human life itself is a major problem. That is why, they say, we feel ill at ease and alienated, as though we are strangers who do not quite fit into our own world. That is also why a haunting malaise troubles the most fortunate among us at the radical core of our being: our pervasive obsession with ourselves. We must, they insist, pass over from our systemic egocentricity to become reoriented about a new focal center.

Consequently, each of these world religions presents itself as a secure and trustworthy *way*. Each way is more than an ennobling concept to raise up the heart; it is also a path that guides behavior and a road that leads to salvation. Jews, therefore, speak of "the way of Torah." Early Christians identified themselves as followers of "the way" (*hodos*). Muslims submit to God's will by following the "straight path" (*shari'ah*) of Islamic religious law. Hindus, with that broad tolerance for which they are famous, present no less than four major "ways" (*margas*) to *moksha* ("liberation"). Buddhists teach the "middle way" (*magga*) to Nibbana (or Nirvana) ("state of being blown out, cool"—that is, liberation from the wheel of rebirth), and some of them refer to each major interpretation of Buddhism as a *yana* ("vehicle").

A Message of Fulfillment

These world religions proclaim ways to personal transformation for those who follow them, despite the affliction of moral evil, physical misery, and death. They announce a message of human fulfillment by which followers may conduct their lives with heartfelt purpose and an uplifting morality by which followers may devote themselves to others with compassionate service. Believers suffer frustrations, disappointments, and failures, of course. Yet each of these religions offers its adherents the strength to pick up the pieces after setbacks, go on in hope, and finally prevail, either within this world or, perhaps, within some further dimension in the future.

Of course, many people are born into a living tradition that nourishes them, and they spontaneously appropriate their parents' religion as their own. Other individuals deliberately choose a particular religion after careful reflection, because it enables them to make sense out of their confusion and wholeness out of their dividedness. They have found its teachings about human dignity and destiny, good and evil, health and pain, life and death to be uniquely persuasive. Both kinds of religious persons confidently root their hopes in a ground that is imperceptible to the senses, yet accessible through faith, enlightenment, or some sort of initiation into a "higher" level of existence. Their own belief system rings true for them and resounds in the deepest recesses of their hearts, while doctrines of other religions appear "less probable."

The Human Predicament

For Jews, Christians, and Muslims, our human problem is the moral ensnarement of *sin* that estranges us from a personal God, but the Creator in faithful and merciful love offers redemption. In Jewish thought, human beings must use their freedom responsibly and make the right choice between two strong inclinations: good tendencies (*yetzer ha tov*) and bad tendencies (*yetzer ha ra*). They must obey the 613 commandments of God's instruction (Torah) in order to confirm their good inclinations and pass from dehumanizing self-will to the ennobling righteousness of God's holy people. In the Christian view, people must struggle against a state of sinfulness that they inherit from their first parents (original sin); they then aggravate this solidarity in sinfulness by their own transgressions (actual, or personal sins). They must by Christ's assistance and empowerment (grace) die to self and pass over with him to resurrection as God's adopted children. In Islamic understanding, human beings must reject the temptations of the devil (Iblis) and choose freely to surrender (Islam) unreservedly to the will of God (Allah) as God's servants and finally, perhaps, as God's friends.

For Hindus and Buddhists, our predicament is not moral but intellectual: We human beings erroneously fail to see things for what they really are, and so we become trapped by the law of karma (action, consequence of an action) on the wheel of endless rebirth. Hindus identify our difficulty as the illusion of individual separateness, the false sentiment that we are discrete selves in our own right, distinct from one another and from the one universal and absolute Self (Brahman-atman). Hindus insist that we all possess the same Self (atman) and that all selfishness is, in fact, based upon pointless error. Therefore, we must adopt one of the approved *margas* and pass over from the state of error that constrains us in rebirth to a liberating realization of our true identity in the universal Self. Buddhists, on the other hand, view our difficulty as the delusion and ignorance of permanent selfhood as such. This ignorance leads to craving desire, and craving desire causes rebirth to further suffering. In fact, the notion of self, whether individual or universal, is empty and void of any reality. Therefore, we must follow the "middle way," with its Noble Eight-fold Path, in order to pass over from our state of ignorance that causes craving desire, rebirth, and suffering to a state of enlightenment and Nibbana. . . .

The Impact of a Sacred Worldview

Religion is the pursuit of transformation under the impact of a sacred worldview. The notion of the sacred is utterly decisive here (although problematical and resistant to discrete analysis), and we must work out at least some general understanding of its meaning. Jews, Christians, Muslims, and Hindus acknowledge the sacred as existing in an ultimate and absolute reality such as God or the Godhead (Brahman-atman). Buddhists recognize the sacred in the ceaseless process or flow of being, although many of them reject any dualistic distinction between the "sacred" and the "profane" (just as the flow of this-worldly experience and absolute Nibbana are really inseparable and the same). All of these religious people further recognize the sacred as an awe-inspiring dimension of whatever symbolizes and/or communicates the *numinous* ("pertaining to the divinely Other"). For example, devotees encounter the numinous in consecrated shrines, seasons of celebration, inspired books, and rites of passage. All religious people experience the sacred as beyond all comprehension, impossible to define, and very difficult to describe. Yet they insist that the sacred is incontestably real, irresistibly attractive, wondrously provocative, and enduringly fascinating. They know that they can approach the sacred only with the utmost reverence.

The sacred transcends every limitation and overflows every boundary. The whole universe cannot fully contain the sacred and its phenomena, because it exceeds our every ordinary horizon. If the ultimately sacred is a divine being, it may be at once deeply *immanent* (abiding within) and absolutely *transcendent* (exceeding limits, transcending). The God of the

Jews, Christians, and Muslims is distinct from all creatures, yet God pervades them all in immanence and surpasses them all in transcendence. For many Hindus, the ultimate divine principle (Brahman-atman), is identified with all things as it pervades them all in immanence and surpasses them all in transcendence. The divinity contains the cosmos, but the cosmos does not contain the divinity.

The Mystery of the Sacred

Since the sacred is intrinsically mysterious, we are incapable of grasping it directly, whether by our senses or by our intellect. Since the sacred exceeds all that we encounter in our natural and ordinary experience, it is *ineffable* (beyond adequate human expression). That is why theological language, for example, can at best be no more than indirect and analogical or negative. Even Thomas Aquinas (1225–74), a philosopher-theologian of extraordinary acumen, affirmed that we know what God is not rather than what God is. Our clouded knowledge of the sacred can be no more than a distant reflection, and our stammering speech about the sacred can be no more than a metaphorical suggestion. Our words may point toward the sacred from afar, but they cannot encompass it. Still, religious people have always tried mentally to probe the meaning of the sacred and have attempted verbally to articulate its significance. They have often created *myths* (vividly imaginative stories) in order to pass on their experience to the next generation. These colorful narratives form the core of their non-written and scriptured traditions, creeds, and texts for worshipping communities.

It is very important to realize that religious persons may persevere in their religiosity whether or not they have any emotional feelings in the presence of the sacred. Religion is not essentially a matter of sensibility and sentiment. Some people are certain that they have somehow encountered the sacred, although they have perceived little or nothing on an

What Belief Demands

To say "I believe . . . in the creator" proclaims, out of the center of my soul, that I know that life is a gift, a responsibility, a venture into human accountability for which there is no excuse acceptable, no justification adequate enough to explain why I did nothing to complete a world given to me for safekeeping. We may, of course, fail because failure is also a mark of creaturehood, the beginning of a growth learned over and over again, from generation to generation, until the end of time. Success is, therefore, not required. We are frail, uncertain. But the outpouring through us of the Breath of God, the spirit that brought each of us into being and sustains us there, is of the essence of God's work on earth. The massacres may go on, the injustices may be legalized, the oppressions may be theologized, the barbarisms may be taken for granted everywhere, but I am expected to meet inhumanity with humanity, human darkness with the gleam of the divine eye at all times, spiritual death with the living Breath of God. I am expected to draw from the Being that is the source of my being so that all of us together may someday, somehow grow to full stature, become that from which we were made, be everything that creaturehood demands.

Joan Chittister,
In Search of Belief, *1999.*

emotional level. Others may engage themselves with enthusiastic and even passionate commitment to the sacred. Even these people recognize, however, that their faith or enlightenment has to sustain them even when all the sweetness of sensible consolation dissolves into the bitter darkness of aridity.

Most religious persons are not mystics who frequently or habitually experience the sacred as immediately available. Some do speak poetically of savoring the supernal delight of the divine presence or hearing the melody of the divine voice. Others recount how the ecstasy of spiritual betrothal has drawn them up out of themselves into the divine embrace. Nevertheless, the vast majority of religious people lead humdrum lives of unspectacular but faithful practice in an earthbound and uninspired context.

Religious people engage in numerous kinds of activities. For example, they likely pray and worship, meditate upon scriptures, engage in ritual celebrations, fast, give alms, go on pilgrimages, or serve the needy—and maintain some sort of contact with the sacred through it all. They all seek to commune with awe-inspiring reality, and they hope that their particular way will lead them to final transformation, enlightenment, or salvation.

The defining dimension of all religious exercises is the sacred connection. Buddhists of the Theravada ("teaching of the elders"—that is, the Buddhism of Southeast Asia), for example, deny the existence of both a personal God and a human soul, yet they are certainly religious, since they acknowledge the sacred. Reform Jews are often agnostic in regard to afterlife, but they too are undeniably religious, since they are committed to the sacred. Members of the Society of Friends (Quakers) and practitioners of Zen give no place to ritual, but they are religious beyond doubt, since they pursue communion with the sacred. Moreover, religious traditions differ from one another in their descriptions of the sacred. They may attempt to speak of the sacred literally, figuratively, or mythically—or not at all. In the last analysis, however, the sacred still remains pivotal and indispensable.

"Science does indeed offer mysteries far more profound than those powered by religion and can point to a highly satisfying meaning to life."

Science Can Uncover Life's Meaning

Wayne Anderson

In the following viewpoint, Wayne Anderson asserts that scientific discovery offers a solid philosophical framework from which to ponder the meaning of life. By offering insights into the nature of matter and humanity's place in the cosmos, science provides the intellectual basis that enables humankind to probe the mysteries of the universe without relying on religious belief. In Anderson's opinion, science connects us to the rest of the universe and reveals that we are part of an intricate web of life—not divinely created masters of the planet. This recognition enables us to embrace nature and seek out meaning and purpose as we evolve, he contends. Anderson teaches physics and astronomy at Sacramento City College in Sacramento, California.

As you read, consider the following questions:

1. What is string theory, according to Wayne Anderson?

Wayne Anderson, "Why Should People Choose Science over Religion?" *Free Inquiry,* vol. 21, Fall 2001, pp. 58–59. Copyright © 2001 The Council for Secular Humanism. Reproduced by permission.

2. In Anderson's opinion, what is one of the major short-comings of revealed religions?

3. Where may our morals and sense of good and evil have stemmed from, according to the author?

The most beautiful experience we can have is the mysterious. It is the fundamental emotion which stands at the cradle of true art and true science. Whoever does not know it and can no longer wonder, no longer marvel, is as good as dead, and his eyes are dimmed. It was the experience of mystery—even if mixed with fear—that engendered religion.

—*Albert Einstein*

Anyone hoping to promote a scientific rather than a religious view of the world absolutely must recognize the extremely valuable and comforting things that religion brings to vast numbers of people. Besides providing a sense of community and moral guidance, religion says there is a meaning to life, and it brings people into contact with the profound mystery of existence. Even in the greatest of tragedies, people find comfort in the belief that someone is in control, even though they do not know his plan. And religion's grappling with the deep mystery of the universe, why it exists and how it came to be, helps to explain why first-rate intellects such as [Isaac] Newton have been so powerfully drawn to it.

What can a scientific view of the world offer people to compete with the comforts bestowed by religion? Can science give meaning to life, and can it envelop people in a sense of deep mystery? I would like to suggest that science does indeed offer mysteries far more profound than those powered by religion and can point to a highly satisfying meaning to life that does not depend on rules laid down by some omnipotent being.

Science and Mystery

In the opening [epigraph], Einstein splendidly captures the sense of awe that accompanies the cutting edge of scientific discovery. The scientist stands in wonder at the incomprehensible majesty of the universe, from the most minute constituents of matter to immense clusters of galaxies to the elegant natural laws that give it all coherence. What are some of these great mysteries of science?

What is matter? The objects of the material world seem so *real*. Yet if we look deeply, this reality begins to fade. The overwhelming majority of each atom—99.9999999999999 percent—is empty space. Probing the protons and neutrons of the atom, we find them also to be nearly total emptiness containing pointlike particles called *quarks*. What, if anything, makes up the quarks? No one knows.[1]

But *why* are there quarks and electrons? Physicists have developed "string theory" to try to explain their existence. According to this idea, the elementary particles arise as vibrations of ten- or eleven-dimensional space-time membranes (called "p-branes"). We do not experience these extra dimensions because they are so tightly curved in on each other that they are beyond our senses. If quarks and electrons have any size at all, it likely comes from the scale of the vibrating p-branes rather than any solid surface. We are left with the disconcerting thought that matter itself may well be an illusion caused by the wiggles of space-time.

What is reality? The Newtonian world of our ordinary senses is a comfortingly rational place. Effect follows cause as time inexorably unfolds. But the deeper realm of quantum mechanics seems an unfathomable mystery. Even in a vacuum, matter pops in and out of existence. Such behavior, called "quantum fluctuations," is not caused by anything, it just happens randomly. Things like electrons are both waves *and* par-

---

1. The same is true of the electron. Although it is not made of quarks, its internal structure (if it has any) is presently unknown.

ticles. This microscopic world of quantum physics is a supreme mystery. How can we visualize an electron as being both a wave and a particle, or matter fluctuating into and out of existence? Quantum mechanics allows us to calculate observable quantities to astonishing precision, so we must take it seriously, but the view of the physical world that it presents us is really incomprehensible.

Ultimate Questions

Countless people have gazed at the blazing night sky and asked where it all came from and perhaps even *why* there is a universe. Such profound questions are at the forefront of modern scientific speculation.

The universe is held together by the four fundamental forces of gravitation, electromagnetism, the weak force, and the strong nuclear force. But why these and no others, and where did they come from? Matter everywhere seems to obey the same fundamental laws, but where did these laws come from, and why do they have their particular form? Were they somehow determined by chance at the beginning of the universe, or is there some underlying reason for them? As Einstein said, "What really interests me is whether God had any choice in the creation of the world."

The universe appears to have begun some twelve to fifteen billion years ago—the so-called Big Bang. But *why* did the Big Bang occur? Some astronomers speculate that new universes (or "multiverses") are being created all the time. If so, are the physical laws in them the same as in our multiverse, or are they totally different? And the most profound mystery of all—why is there a universe in the first place? *Why is there something rather than nothing?*

Can Science Give Our Lives Meaning?

If by "meaning" we expect science to reveal that a superior power is directing our lives, the answer is no. There is no credible evidence for such a guiding force. However, science can show us how we fit into the fabric of the universe. It can reveal how deeply we are embedded in nature, rather than being special creations. Science can provide us with the raw materials—the knowledge—but we human beings must devise our own purpose. Science will not *replace* religion. Rather it will be a major part of the intellectual basis of whatever worldview does replace it. The failure to recognize that humans are indeed a part of nature is one of the great shortcomings of revealed religions.

I would suggest that three branches of science are especially relevant in providing a basis on which to devise meaning for ourselves. These are astronomy, evolutionary biology, and ecological environmentalism.

Astronomy

Astronomy connects us to the rest of the universe. It shows us that we live on a small planet orbiting a middle-aged yellow dwarf star near the outer edge of a spiral galaxy, one of billions of other such galaxies. Armed with such knowledge, it is difficult to think of ourselves as special beings holding central importance in the eyes of some creator.

Astronomy also reveals that we came from the stars. The atoms of our bodies, and everything else on Earth, were fused in the nuclear infernos of generations of stars before our solar system even existed. Near the ends of their lives, these stars blew those atoms out into space, where they mixed with vast gas clouds out of which stars and planets—and us—are born. As [American astronomer] Carl Sagan often said, we are stardust. But the story does not end here. About five billion years from now, our sun will swell to become a red giant, expelling some of its matter, including that of the vaporized planets, back into space, there to mix with more gas clouds to continue the cycle of star birth. Not only did we come from the stars, but we will eventually return to the stars.

The Beauty and Power of Science

To discover that the universe is some 8 to 15 billion and not 6 to 12 thousand years old improves our appreciation of its sweep and grandeur; to entertain the notion that we are a particularly complex arrangement of atoms, and not some breath of divinity, at the very least enhances our respect for atoms; to discover, as now seems probable, that our planet is one of billions of other worlds in the Milky Way Galaxy and that our galaxy is one of billions more, majestically expands the arena of what is possible; to find that our ancestors were also the ancestors of apes ties us to the rest of life and makes possible important—if occasionally rueful—reflections on human nature.

Plainly there is no way back. Like it or not, we are stuck with science. We had better make the best of it. When we finally come to terms with it and fully recognize its beauty and its power, we will find, in spiritual as well as in practical matters, that we have made a bargain strongly in our favor.

Carl Sagan,
Skeptical Inquirer, *March/April 1996.*

Lest one think that this is just sterile scientific knowledge, consider the case of a close friend of mine who died of AIDS. As his body was succumbing to the disease, and, as he struggled to accept his approaching death, he explained that he was returning to the universe. He certainly did not welcome his death—neither do religious folk—but he recognized it as part of a vast cosmic cycle. Surely such knowledge makes the end of life easier to accept than fear of eternal torment.

Evolutionary Biology

If astronomy shows us that our atoms were forged in the stars, evolutionary biology tells us how these building blocks came to be shaped into us, by the same process that led to all other living things. We are no special creation, but rather a product of the natural processes that produced the myriad variety of living things on Earth.

But we must not stop with the evolution of our bodies. Not only are our brains a product of natural selection, but according to the emerging field of evolutionary psychology, so are some of the *thoughts* that are formed by those brains. Our morals and our sense of good and evil may have evolved subject to the pressures of natural selection. They are not universal absolutes handed down by a divine being.

Once we accept that our morals may have evolved, we have the dazzling freedom to change them as necessary, without the fear of divine wrath. Although our notions of proper behavior must have had survival value early in our evolution, some of them have lost that value and should be abandoned. An apt case is the vehement religious condemnation of "deviant" sexuality. When making as many babies as possible was vital to the survival of the tribe, it made sense to discourage other sexual outlets. But when we probably have more people than Earth can comfortably carry and modern medicine ensures the survival of most infants, what is the problem with nonprocreative sex?

Of course many people, even nonreligious ones, find repugnant the notion that there is no absolute good and evil. It seems to open the door to the worst kinds of moral relativism. However, science does seem to be pointing in that direction. As Robert Wright observed in *The Moral Animal*, the truth can make you free, but it may not make you happy. Nevertheless, we do ourselves no good by pretending that the morals of the past carry unassailable authority. If we are to survive in the future, we must be ready to modify our ideas of right and wrong to fit a world vastly different from the one in which we evolved.

Ecological Environmentalism

We share this planet with millions of other life forms, all of which evolved as we did. We were given no special dominion over other life. Yet throughout human history, people treated every single thing on Earth as though it was put here solely for our use. Other species exploit their environment as best they can, but we are much better at it. And therein lies the problem: We are *too* efficient at it.

Sometime near the middle of the twentieth century, human beings began to comprehend fully the enormous extent to which technological society was usurping Earth. In the past few decades, many of us have come to think of ourselves as participants in, rather than masters of, the intricate web of life on this planet. This view has spread to much of the world and will not go away. We now ask of things like housing developments, scientific projects, and even international treaties: How will this affect the environment? The environment may not always come out on top, but it has become an important player. As human society continues to reform itself, environmentalism will gain even greater importance as a secular principle guiding our choices.

By themselves scientific discoveries do not give humans a purpose in life. But they do anchor us firmly in the natural processes of the universe. They can provide the philosophical and intellectual framework from which to chart our own course through the cosmos. Such a voyage may be terrifying, but it can also be exhilarating!

> *"In the skies themselves, and in what cosmologists are learning about them, the armies of the mind and the forces of the spirit are searching for common ground."*

Both Religion and Science Can Reveal Life's Meaning

Sharon Begley

Science and religion have often clashed, most notably since Charles Darwin published his theory of evolution in the nineteenth century, notes Sharon Begley in the following viewpoint. The scientist's understanding of life as the result of chemical reactions and natural selection seemed to conflict with the religious believer's view of life as a divine creation. By the end of the twentieth century, however, a growing number of specialists were seeing scientists and people of faith engaged in a mutually supportive quest for understanding. Many believe that recent scientific theories point to the existence of an ultimate reality or supreme being and that both science and faith can enhance the human sense of connection to the cosmos. Begley, an award-winning science writer, is a senior editor at Newsweek *magazine.*

Sharon Begley, *The Hand of God: Thoughts and Images Reflecting the Spirit of the Universe*, West Conshohocken, PA: Lionheart Books, 1999. Copyright © 1999 Lionheart Books, Ltd. Reproduced by permission of Templeton Foundation Press.

As you read, consider the following questions:

1. According to Sharon Begley, what is Walt Whitman's complaint in his poem about the "learn'd astronomer"?

2. What conclusions did astronomer Alan Sandage's research lead him to, according to the author?

3. What comment did Albert Einstein, quoted by the author, make about science and religion?

The age of naked-eye astronomy has lasted for most of our time on Earth: If the length of humankind's 2.5 million-year tenure is taken as one 24-hour day, then the era of the telescope has lasted a mere 15 seconds. Throughout the other 23 hours, 59 minutes and 45 seconds, our unaided eyes could no more penetrate the veils covering the secrets of the universe than the flash of a firefly could penetrate the canopy of stars that unfurled above us every cloudless night. Few people realized that, beyond the visible stars and moon and occasional planet, there lay worlds and worlds without end. But even though we could see no farther than the frontispiece of the universe, in the years before telescopes the cosmos still drew us. It was the stuff of eternity, infinity—as unbounded as humankind's imagination.

Come, the stars invited; lie supine at the top of a hill on a night when neither the glow of the moon nor a roof of clouds interferes with your view of the sky, in a place where the lights of human habitation are too dim to wash out the view. Look up. There, where the Pleiades burn. Or there—where Orion stretches so boldly over the southern sky. And everywhere, where the uncounted and uncountable hosts prick the black velvet. Look. Stare. Maybe the indifferent heavens will offer a sign, however small, that there is a world beyond the world we see, that there is meaning in the void and a harmony between the mind of man and the limitless reaches of space.

Closing the gaps of that limitless reach have been the 20th century's high-powered telescopes. Namesake of Hubble, remote offspring of Galileo, today's space-based machinery bring us images so far beyond what we could ever imagine that they have changed dramatically our view of the heavens and the origins of the universe. And yet, ironically, the more focused the portraits from deep space, the more meticulous and specific our calculations, the more it seems improbable, even impossible, that our world could have been an arbitrary occurrence.

The majesty of the heavens and their regularity—the cycling of the seasons, the rhythm of day and night—inspire a suspicion that we simply cannot be looking at some meaningless accident. How fitting, then, that it is in cosmology—the scientific study of the beginning and evolution of the universe—where the stage is set for a historic reconciliation of those two rivals for man's awe: science and religion. In the skies themselves, and in what cosmologists are learning about them, the armies of the mind and the forces of the spirit are searching for common ground.

Science Versus Religion

To appreciate the seismic change taking place in the relationship between science and faith, one need only recall how deeply the rift between the two has become part of our culture. Walt Whitman captured it best when he wrote in the poem that was to become part of *Leaves of Grass*,

> When I heard the learn'd astronomer,
> When the proofs, the figures, were
> ranged in columns before me
> When I was shown the charts and
> the diagrams, to add, divide, and
> measure them;

When I, sitting, heard the astronomer,
where he lectured with much applause
in the lecture-room,

How soon, unaccountable, I became
tired and sick;

Till rising and gliding out, I wander'd
off by myself,

In the mystical moist night-air, and
from time to time,

Look'd up in perfect silence at the stars.

Whitman was not alone when he complained that "the learn'd astronomer's" discoveries had spoiled the mystery and romance of the stars; his poem describes the science most of us know. It is a science that has, traditionally, encroached on the terrain of religion, offering a natural (and often dry) explanation for what had previously been regarded as wondrous and even supernatural. It is a science that obliterates mysteries and replaces them with a differential equation. It is a science that addresses totally different questions than religion: Science explains the world, God is behind the world; science explains what is, religion offers a sense of what ought to be; science tells us how the world acts, religion tells us how we should act.

And yet it was not always so. For most of the previous 2,000 years, science and religion were engaged in a common quest for understanding, each taking strength from the other.

Science as an Avenue to Faith

Until the middle of the 19th century, science was perceived not as antithetical to faith but rather as an avenue to deeper faith and to greater appreciation for the works of the Creator. In nature, scientists believed, could be discerned the handiwork of God.

The leading lights of the Scientific Revolution were men of faith as well as men of science. Early astronomers like Tycho Brahe and Johannes Kepler, devout Christians both, studied the motions of the planets and believed that in so doing, they were getting a peek at the blueprints that God had drawn for the universe. Isaac Newton did not doubt that in uncovering the laws of motion and universal gravitation, he was being granted a glimpse of the operating manual of the vast machine called Creation that God had assembled and kept running.

These early scientists trusted that their inquiries would yield knowledge because they believed that God had created a rational, ordered world, a world governed by laws and not by chaos or divine whim, a world in which discoveries therefore had universal meaning: If an apple fell *here* for one reason, then that reason applied throughout the universe. The world was not an endless sequence of unique cases. Without the confidence that there existed a consistent, rational, eternal set of principles governing nature, there wouldn't be much point in doing science—whose goal is, after all, the uncovering of the regularities of nature that we have come to call laws.

In the 17th century, science and religion signed a sort of mutual nonaggression treaty, in which each vowed to refrain from spreading into the domain of the other. For science, this move was defensive: By declaring outright that its discoveries did not, and could not, be used as tools to undermine belief, science was declaring that it operated in a domain parallel to rather than overlapping that where religion reigned. This was partly a reaction to how the Church had treated Galileo.[1] If science took the position that its discoveries did not speak to the truth or falsity of religion, there would be no more—or at least, less excuse for—putting scientists under house arrest. For faith, a nonaggression treaty also offered protection: By

---

1. In 1616 Italian astronomer Galileo Galilei was placed under lifelong house arrest for supporting the theory of a sun-centered solar system. This theory conflicted with the religious dogma of the time.

asserting that it spoke to realities beyond the reach of science, it effectively inoculated itself from any surprise discoveries that might otherwise be interpreted as undermining its teachings.

The Rise of Science

But the rise of science had already brought with it Copernicus's sun-centered solar system, which knocked Earth from the center of creation. Next came Newton's physics, which made the universe an inanimate wind-up machine. The Enlightenment's focus on reason as the supreme human power, its philosophies of reductionism and materialism, and its rejection of authority and revelation and text, were all antithetical to religion. The truce was fraying.

In 1859 Charles Darwin published, in *On the Origin of Species*, his theory of evolutionary biology, which seemed to dethrone the Creator and replace him with blind chance. Darwin more than any scientist before dislodged humans from the apex of the tree of life, making them seem almost incidental to Creation, an afterthought, some meaningless bits of carbon chemistry dotting an insignificant planet orbiting an ordinary star way out in the hinterland of a galaxy indistinguishable from the other 100 billion galaxies believed to fill the universe. The biologist's view of life as a series of complex chemical reactions did not lie easily with the theologian's idea of life as a divine gift; if everything from the creation of the planets to the eruption of a volcano to the leukemia that takes the life of a child is seen as having, in fact or in theory, a natural cause and explanation, then it seemed like there was no room left for God to act in the world. Darwin's theory of evolution through natural selection was arguably the single event that allowed the supposedly unbridgeable chasm between God and science to attain the status of iconic truth.

From the mid-19th century on, the relationship between science and faith deteriorated into one of animosity, at least in the West. True, some theologians made their peace with modern science: One American clergyman welcomed Darwin's theory of evolution through chance and natural selection because that view implied that God had created a world that could and did make itself. This was a gift of love, the clergyman argued, allowing the creation to have independence rather than making it a divine puppet theater. But few men of God saw Darwin's theory in any such positive light. Instead, most other theologians began to identify science as the enemy, as a hostile force invading and laying waste to the sacred. . . .

A Pointless Universe?

With the scythe of science slashing away at all evidence of the divine, no wonder so many people have come to view science as nihilistic, as threatening, as undermining their hope that there is meaning in their lives, as replacing a sense of being unique and God-created with an existential void. This view was famously summed up by Nobel Prize–winning physicist Steven Weinberg, who concluded, "The more the universe seems comprehensible, the more it seems pointless."

Or maybe not. There is another interpretation of the understanding we have achieved. This view holds, contrary to Weinberg, that humankind's very ability to comprehend the universe suggests a profound connection, heretofore lost, between the mind of man and the works of God. Just as science once threatened faith, now it is—at least for some—restoring faith by offering this solace. For others, science is at least serving a function that faith alone once did: making humans feel connected to, not alienated from, creation.

The aspect of science that offers this hope is so basic that it is like [poet Edgar Allan] Poe's purloined letter: Right under our noses, we overlook it. This is the remarkable fact that the human mind can do science in the first place—that it can, in other words, figure out the world. Science works. Lights turn on when we flick a switch; buildings stand; water boils when we heat it; planets show up in the predicted place in space when we send robotic emissaries to them.

Why should this be so? "The magic of science is that we can understand at least part of nature—perhaps in principle all of it—using the scientific method of inquiry," says astronomer and physicist Paul Davies, winner of the Templeton Prize for advancing religion. Why, Davies asks, should the laws of nature be comprehensible and accessible to humans? It could, of course, be just a quirk, a coincidence, with no deeper meaning. Or, it could say something purely scientific—though we don't know, precisely, what—about the kind of beings that emerge from nature: As children of what Davies calls "the cosmic order," perhaps it is inevitable that their minds should "reflect that order in their cognitive capabilities."

Some scientists and theologians suspect, however, that the harmony between the intellectual ability of man and the laws of nature reflects something more profound. It need not be anything so simplistic as, "God made the world, and God made me, so He made me able to understand the rest of His Creation." It is, instead, one of those places where a scientific discovery—that the universe can be fathomed by the mind of man—serves a function that, once, only religion could. To wit: a sense of connectedness between humans and the cosmos. . . .

Alan Sandage's Observations

One scientist whose research led him to faith is Alan Sandage, the astronomer who has spent the better part of the past forty years at the great telescopes on Mt. Wilson and Las Campanas Observatories. Sandage inherited the mantle of Edwin Hubble, who in 1929 discovered that the universe is expanding, rushing out like a tide and carrying along with it galaxies and nebulas like so much flotsam and jetsam upon the waves of

Tinged with Mysticism

After close on two centuries of passionate struggles, neither science nor faith has succeeded in discrediting its adversary. On the contrary, it becomes obvious that neither can develop normally without the other. And the reason is simple: The same life animates both. Neither in its impetus nor its achievements can science go to its limits without becoming tinged with mysticism and charged with faith.

Pierre Teilhard de Chardin,
The Phenomenon of Man, *1959.*

space-time. After Hubble's death in 1953, Sandage assumed the task of measuring the fate of the universe.

To do so, Sandage observed two kinds of stars: exploded stars called supernovas and variable stars called Cepheids, whose period of variation in brightness and intrinsic luminosity are precisely related. Sandage determined the distance to these stars by the shift in their light spectra, and calculated their recession velocity. The relationship between those two numbers would reveal whether the universe would expand forever or, one day, stop and reverse course, hurtling toward a Big Crunch. For the insights they gave him into the design of the cosmos, Sandage called the photographic plates that he and others made at Palomar's telescopes "the plates of Moses."

As much as any other 20th-century astronomer, Sandage actually figured out the Creation: His observations showed how old the universe is (15 billion years or so) and that it is expanding just fast enough to do so forever. But throughout it all Sandage was nagged by mysteries whose answers were not to be found in the glittering supernovas. Among them: Why is there something rather than nothing? He began to despair of answering such questions through reason alone. "It was my science that drove me to the conclusion that the world is much more complicated than can be explained by science," he says. "It is only through the supernatural that I can understand the mystery of existence."

The Mystery of Quantum Mechanics

Some scientists who study not the macro-world of astronomy but the micro-world of particles smaller than an atom have been similarly moved. Quantum mechanics, the branch of physics that describes events at the subatomic level, is a consistent, empirically proved framework that predicts how subatomic particles behave and interact. But it is also "spooky," to use Einstein's description. His most famous experiment in this regard is so odd that, when Einstein devised it with two collaborators as a thought experiment in 1935, he called it a paradox. It goes like this. Let's say that a radioactive atom decays. In so doing, it emits a pair of particles. The particles are linked forever in this way: The laws of nature dictate that if one of the particles is spinning in a way that we can call clockwise, then the other particle is spinning counterclockwise.

Now, let's say that you measure the spin of one of the particles. It turns up clockwise. By this very act of measurement, then, you have *determined* the spin of the other particle—even if it is at the other end of the universe. Einstein called this "spooky action at the distance," but it has been proved right time and again. What happens, according to physicists' current interpretation, is that each particle exists in two states simultaneously, somehow spinning clockwise and counterclockwise at the same time. Only when an observer makes a measurement on one particle does that particle settle down and choose one spin. This choice affects which spin its partner chooses. This suggests to some scholars a level of reality beyond the familiar

Science and Religion

Science wants to know the mechanism of the universe, religion the meaning. The two cannot be separated. Many scientists feel there is no place in research for discussion of anything that sounds mystical. But it is unreasonable to think we already know enough about the natural world to be confident about the totality of forces.

Charles H. Townes, physicist, 1964 Nobel Prize winner.

everyday one, a reality in which spatial distance is meaningless (because the second particle receives the information about the first particle's choice simultaneously and makes its own choice based on that instantaneously). It is in this other level of reality that some find a place for the existence of a supreme being.

A Restored Sense of Wonder

Twentieth-century discoveries in astronomy and cosmology—"the charts and the diagrams," to say nothing of the formulas and calculations—are not sending us "tired and sick," fleeing like Whitman back into the mysteries of "the moist night" to take refuge in our ignorance. Instead, astronomers' findings—both the new nebulae and novas and galaxies they spy with their telescopes and the inferences they draw about the orbs scattered across the universe—are restoring a sense of wonder, and even of purpose, in a world at times hostile to both. Instead of leaving less and less room for a Creator who, at least once, acted in the world, they are acting as an inspiration to and support for faith.

This is a momentous switch. Science has been pilloried for centuries for robbing the world of its enigmatic beauty and for squeezing God out of the picture. Like kudzu creeping over the landscape of the South, it spread into the realm of religion until there was not a patch of territory that religion could claim as its own. Finally, science, the bogeyman of faith, is undergoing a radical change in its place in human culture. . . .

The discoveries that come streaming in from our telescopes are inspiring thoughtful people not to subsume science to faith or faith to science, but to seek an accommodation between the two. It is this quest that is winning adherents as the millennium begins. Science and religion illuminate different mysteries, all agree, casting their light on different questions. But each can heal the worst excesses of the other, with science, as Pope John Paul II said, "Purify[ing] religion from error and superstition," and religion "purify[ing] science from idolatry and false absolutes" by infusing it with a little humility. Or, as Einstein observed, "Science without religion is lame, religion without science is blind."

Two Ways of Looking at the World

The new scholarship of science and theology suggests, too, that they have one thing in common: the motivation that animates both in the search for scientific truths and the search for spiritual meaning. "I think that fundamentally the impetus for the two quests is the same," says Carl Feit, a biologist and practicing Jew. "Religion and science are two ways of looking at the world, and each helps guide our search for understanding. Profoundly religious people are asking the same questions as profound scientists: Who are we? And what are we? What's the purpose? What's the end? Where do we come from? And where are we going? We have this need, this desire, this drive, to understand ourselves and the world that we live in."

When Václav Havel, the poet and president of the Czech Republic, received the Liberty Medal in Philadelphia on the 218th anniversary of the Declaration of Independence, he described the societal transition underway in the world. Science, he said, has become alienated from the lives we lead. For too long it has failed "to connect with the most intrinsic nature of reality and with natural human experience. It is now more a source of disintegration and doubt than a source of integration and meaning." But he saw a glimmer of hope. "Paradoxically, inspiration for the renewal of this lost integrity can once again be found in science . . . a science producing ideas that in a certain sense allow it to transcend its own limits. . . . Transcendence is the only real alternative to extinction," especially the extinction of the collective human soul. That was in 1994. Now, as the millennium turns, Havel's hope that science would cease to be a source of doubt and become a source of inspiration is becoming realized.

At the end of the 20th century, it is in what science is unearthing about nature that we are seeing confirmation of existing religious beliefs or inspiration for a whole new kind of faith. We are not fusing religion and science; the two will always retain their separate identities. But from scholars to churchgoers to those who have turned their backs on organized religion, we are seeking and finding today in the discoveries of science—and especially in the discoveries of astronomy and cosmology—what in eras past only religion has offered: solace and support. A sense of connection between the otherwise insignificant human mind and the tapestry of creation. A sense of wonder, and of awe; a sense that the world is rational; a sense, even, of the sacred. And, to believers, hints of the nature and character of God.

OPPOSING
VIEWPOINTS®
SERIES

CHAPTER 3

What Motivates Moral Behavior?

Chapter Preface

The news is usually brimming with stories revealing the questionable state of ethics and morals in today's world. From lying politicians and corrupt corporate practices to serial killers and genocidal wars, humankind seems to have an inexhaustible capacity for deceit and brutality. And yet even amidst such callousness, we also encounter great heroism, generosity, kindness, and honesty. Many would agree that humans have the potential to commit both good and evil. But how do we come to define what is "good" and "evil"? What enables us to choose between right and wrong?

In the first viewpoint of this chapter, Christian editor and author Philip Yancey contends that humans must look beyond themselves to a higher authority for moral guidance. He believes that God and religion, which provides a way to commune with God, constitute moral authority. In his view, basic ethical principles are unchanging and absolute because they have been established by an absolute being, the creator of the universe. Without God, Yancey argues, we are left with the "collective sentiments of human beings" as a guide to morality, a situation that leaves us "vulnerable to dangerous swings of moral consensus." Frank R. Zindler, editor of *American Atheist* magazine, strongly disagrees with Yancey. Zindler maintains that morality is rooted in the long-term process of human evolution and cultural development. What we now define as ethical conduct is largely learned behavior that has ensured the survival of the human species over millions of years, he writes. Zindler views morality as a product of nature. In his opinion, religion is a primitive cultural adaptation that served us earlier in our evolutionary development, but should now be replaced with reason.

The other authors in this chapter do not attempt to define the source of morality but rather examine worldviews and dispositions that they believe promote genuinely moral behavior. For example, humanist, editor, and author Paul Kurtz describes several of the principles espoused by secular humanists. Secular humanism is a philosophy that celebrates reason, freedom of thought, and individual liberty while rejecting supernaturalism and religious dogma. Kurtz maintains that rational deliberation allows us to discern what is ethical without having to rely on religious laws and authorities. Conversely, professor and author John Gray argues that secular humanism suppresses humanity's natural impulse toward religious belief. Instincts, he points out, cannot be repressed without negative consequences. Gray believes that repressed religion eventually reasserts itself in dangerous ways, resulting in tyrannies and mass atrocities.

Finally, lecturer and critic Alfie Kohn contends that altruism—an attitude of selfless concern for others—is at the root of the ability to help other people. Kohn argues that altruism stems from an inherent capacity for empathy and connectedness. This capacity, however, must be developed through life experiences and encouragement from the surrounding culture. On the other hand, philosopher and teacher Tibor R. Machan maintains that effective moral behavior begins with self-concern. Those who have first taken care of their own needs are better able to offer assistance to others, Machan argues. He believes that the "self-sacrificing" disposition of altruism is impractical because one who does not help himself cannot successfully help others.

Philosophers, religious believers, and scientists have widely varying opinions on the origins of morality and what mental attitudes and cultural influences promote ethical behavior. The following chapter presents several of these disparate views.

"Historically, [civilization] has always relied on religion to provide a source for . . . moral authority."

Morality Requires Religious Belief

Philip Yancey

In the following viewpoint, Philip Yancey contends that true morality is rooted in a belief in God. According to Yancey, contemporary secular society has reduced the notion of morality to a question of personal choice, causing a general decline in ethics. He maintains that the ability to make authentic judgments about right and wrong requires the guidance of religion; any moral system established by nonbelievers is completely arbitrary since it has no higher authority as its foundation. Yancey is the editor-at-large of Christianity Today *magazine and the author of several books, including* Reaching for the Invisible God *and* What's So Amazing About Grace?

As you read, consider the following questions:

1. How does Philip Yancey define "unmorality"?

2. What are the symptoms of moral illness in the United States, according to Yancey?

Philip Yancey, "Nietzsche Was Right," *Books & Culture*, January/February 1998. Copyright © 1998 by Philip Yancey.

3. According to James Davison Hunter, cited by the author, what happens to a society that loses all moral consensus?

A representative of Generation X named Sam told me he had been discovering the strategic advantages of truth. As an experiment, he decided to stop lying. "It helps people picture you and relate to you more reliably," he said. "Truth can be positively beneficial in many ways."

I asked what would happen if he found himself in a situation where it would prove *more* beneficial for him to lie. He said he would have to judge the context, but he was trying to prefer not lying.

For Sam, the decision to lie or tell the truth involved not morality, but a social construct to be adopted or rejected as a matter of expedience. In essence, the source of moral authority for Sam is himself, and that in a nutshell is the dilemma confronting moral philosophy in the postmodern world.

The Rise of Unmorality

Something unprecedented in human history is brewing: a rejection of external moral sources altogether. Individuals and societies have always been immoral to varying degrees. Individuals (never an entire society) have sometimes declared themselves amoral, professing agnosticism about ethical matters. Only recently, however, have serious thinkers entertained the notion of unmorality: that there is no such thing as morality. A trend prefigured by [philosopher Friedrich] Nietzsche, prophesied by [writer Fyodor] Dostoyevsky, and analyzed presciently by C.S. Lewis in *The Abolition of Man* is now coming to fruition. The very concept of morality is undergoing a profound change, led in part by the advance guard of a new science called "evolutionary psychology."

So far, however, the pioneers of unmorality have practiced a blatant contradiction. Following in the style of [philosopher] Jean-Paul Sartre, who declared that meaningful communication is impossible even as he devoted his life to communicating meaningfully, the new moralists first proclaim that morality is capricious, perhaps even a joke, then proceed to use moral categories to condemn their opponents. These new high priests lecture us solemnly about multiculturalism, gender equality, homophobia, and environmental degradation, all the while ignoring the fact that they have systematically destroyed any basis for judging such behavior right or wrong. The emperor so quick to discourse about fashion happens to be stark naked. . . .

In a great irony, the "politically correct" movement defending the rights of women, minorities, and the environment often positions itself as an enemy of the Christian church when, in historical fact, the church has contributed the very underpinnings that make such a movement possible. Christianity brought an end to slavery, and its crusading fervor also fueled the early labor movement, women's suffrage, human rights campaigns, and civil rights. According to [sociologist] Robert Bellah, "there has not been a major issue in the history of the United States on which religious bodies did not speak out, publicly and vociferously."

It was no accident that Christians pioneered in the antislavery movement, for their beliefs had a theological impetus. Both slavery and the oppression of women were based, anachronistically, on an embryonic form of Darwinism. Aristotle had observed that

> Tame animals are naturally better than wild animals, yet for all tame animals there is an advantage in being under human control, as this secures their survival. And as regards the relationship between male and female, the former is naturally superior, the latter inferior, the former rules and the latter is subject. By analogy, the same must necessarily apply to mankind as a whole. Therefore all men who differ from one another by as much as the soul differs from the

body or man from a wild beast (and that is the state of those who work by using their bodies, and for whom that is the best they can do)—these people are slaves by nature, and it is better for them to be subject to this kind of control, as it is better for the other creatures I have mentioned.... It is clear that there are certain people who are free and certain people who are slaves by nature, and it is both to their advantage, and just, for them to be slaves.... From the hour of their birth, some men are marked out for subjection, others for rule.

Cross out the name *Aristotle* and read the paragraph again as the discovery of a leading evolutionary psychologist. No one is proposing the reimposition of slavery, of course—but why not? If we learn our morality from nature, and if our only rights are those we create for ourselves, why should not the strong exercise their "natural rights" over the weak?

The Need for a Moral Authority

As Alasdair MacIntyre remarks in *After Virtue*, modern protesters have not abandoned moral argument, though they have abandoned any coherent platform from which to make a moral argument. They keep using moral terminology—it is *wrong* to own slaves, rape a woman, abuse a child, despoil the environment, discriminate against homosexuals—but they have no "higher authority" to which to appeal to make their moral judgments. MacIntyre concludes,

Hence the *utterance* of protest is characteristically addressed to those who already *share* the protestors' premises. The effects of incommensurability ensure that protestors rarely have anyone else to talk to but themselves. This is not to say that protest cannot be effective; it is to say that it cannot be *rationally* effective and that its dominant modes of expression give evidence of a certain perhaps unconscious awareness of this.

In the United States, we prefer to settle major issues on utilitarian or pragmatic grounds. But philosophers including

Aristotle and David Hume argued powerfully in favor of slavery on those very grounds. Hitler pursued his genocidal policies against the Jews and "defective" persons on utilitarian grounds. Unless modern thinkers can locate a source of moral authority somewhere else than in the collective sentiments of human beings, we will always be vulnerable to dangerous swings of moral consensus. . . .

A Generation of Wingless Chickens

> It is easy to see that the moral sense has been bred out of certain sections of the population, like the wings have been bred off certain chickens to produce more white meat on them. This is a generation of wingless chickens.
>
> *—Flannery O'Connor*

What happens when an entire society becomes populated with wingless chickens? I need not dwell on the contemporary symptoms of moral illness in the United States: Our rate of violent crime has quintupled in my lifetime; a third of all babies are now born out of wedlock; half of all marriages end in divorce; the richest nation on earth has a homeless population larger than the entire population of some nations. These familiar symptoms are just that, symptoms. A diagnosis would look beyond them to our loss of a teleological sense. "Can one be a saint if God does not exist? That is the only concrete problem I know of today," wrote Albert Camus in *The Fall*.

Civilization holds together when a society learns to place moral values above the human appetites for power, wealth, violence, and pleasure. Historically, it has always relied on religion to provide a source for that moral authority. In fact, according to [historians] Will and Ariel Durant, "There is no significant example in history, before our time, of a society successfully maintaining moral life without the aid of religion." They added the foreboding remark, "The greatest question of our time is not communism versus individualism, not

Europe versus America, not even the East versus the West; it is whether men can live without God."

[Playwright and former president of Czechoslovakia] Václav Havel, a survivor of a civilization that tried to live without God, sees the crisis clearly:

> I believe that with the loss of God, man has lost a kind of absolute and universal system of coordinates, to which he could always relate everything, chiefly himself: His world and his personality gradually began to break up into separate, incoherent fragments corresponding to different, relative, coordinates.

On moral issues—social justice, sexuality, marriage and family, definitions of life and death—society badly needs a moral tether, or "system of coordinates" in Havel's phrase. Otherwise, our laws and politics will begin to reflect the same kind of moral schizophrenia already seen in individuals.

On what moral basis do doctrinaire Darwinians, committed to the survival of the fittest, ask us to protect the environment, in effect lending a hand to those we make "unfit"? On what basis do abortionists denounce the gender-based abortion practiced in India, where, in some cities, 99 percent of abortions involve a female fetus? (For this reason, some Indian cities have made it illegal for doctors to reveal to parents a fetus's gender after an ultrasound test.) Increasingly, the schizophrenia of personal morality is being projected onto society at large.

James Davison Hunter recounts watching a segment of *The Phil Donahue Show* featuring men who left their wives and then had affairs with those wives' mothers. Some of the relationships failed, but some worked out fine, the men reported. A psychologist sitting on the panel concluded, "The important thing to remember is that there is no right or wrong. I hear no wrongdoing. As I listen to their stories, I hear pain."

Clay Butler/www.sidewalkbubblegum.com.

The Fate of a Godless Society

Hunter speculates where a society might be headed once it loses all moral consensus. "Personally I'm into ritual animal sacrifice," says one citizen. "Oh, really," says another. "I happen to be into man-boy relationships." "That's great," responds a third, "but my preference is . . ." and so on. The logical end of such thinking, Hunter suggests, can be found in the Marquis de Sade's novel *Juliette*, which declares, "Nothing is forbidden by nature."

In Sade's novel, Juliette's lover enhances their sexual ecstasy by raping Juliette's daughter and throwing the girl into a fire; wielding a poker, the mother herself prevents the child's escape. A brute accused of raping, sodomizing, and murdering more than two dozen boys, girls, men, and women defends himself by saying that all concepts of virtue and vice are arbitrary; self-interest is the paramount rule:

> Justice has no real existence, it is the deity of every passion. . . . So let us abandon our belief in this fiction, it no more exists than does the God of whom fools believe it the image; there is no God in this world, neither is there virtue, neither is there justice; there is nothing good, useful, or necessary but our passions.

U.S. courts today take pains to decide the merits of a case apart from religion or natural law. New York State passed a law prohibiting the use of children in pornographic films and, in order to protect it from civil libertarians, specified that the law is based not on moral or religious reasons, rather on "mental health" grounds. In earlier times the Supreme Court appealed to the "general consent" of society's moral values in deciding issues such as polygamy. I wonder on what possible grounds the Court might rule against polygamy today (practiced in 84 percent of all recorded cultures)—or incest, or pederasty, for that matter. All these moral taboos derive from a religious base; take away that foundation, and why should the practices be forbidden?

To ask a basic question, What sense does marriage make in a morally neutral society? A friend of mine, though gay, is nevertheless troubled by calls for gay marriages. "What's to keep two brothers from marrying, if they declare a commitment to each other?" he asks. "They could then enjoy the tax breaks and advantages of inheritance and health plans. It seems to me something more should be at stake in an institution like marriage." Yes, but *what* is at stake in marriage? The authors of *Habits of the Heart* found that few individuals in their survey except committed Christians could explain why they stayed married to their spouses. Marriage as a social construct is arbitrary, flexible, and open to redefinition. Marriage as a sacrament established by God is another matter entirely.

Separating Sex from Morality

Feminist thinkers have led the way in questioning the traditional basis of sexual ethics. In *The Erotic Silence of the American Wife*, Dalma Heyn argues that women unnaturally bind themselves at the marriage altar, abandoning their true needs and desires. Heyn recommends extramarital affairs as the cure for what she sardonically calls "the Donna Reed syndrome."[1] In an essay in *Time*, Barbara Ehrenreich celebrated the fact that "Sex can finally, after all these centuries, be separated from the all-too-serious business of reproduction. . . . The only ethic that can work in an overcrowded world is one that insists that . . . sex—preferably among affectionate and consenting adults—belongs squarely in the realm of play."

Ehrenreich and Heyn are detaching sex from any teleological meaning invested in it by religion. But why limit the experience to affectionate and consenting adults? If sex is a matter of play, why not sanction pederasty, as did the Greeks and Romans? Why choose the age of 18—or 16, or 14, or 12—to mark an arbitrary distinction between child abuse and indulging in play? If sex is mere play, why do we prosecute people for incest? (Indeed, the Sex Information and Education Council of the United States circulated a paper expressing skepticism regarding "moral and religious pronouncements with respect to incest," lamenting that the taboo has hindered scientific investigation.)

The Alice-in-Wonderland world of untethered ethics has little place for traditional morality. When California adopted a sex education program, the American Civil Liberties Union (ACLU) sent this official memorandum:

1. A reference to a 1960s television show featuring a traditional suburban wife and mother.

The ACLU regrets to inform you of our opposition to SB 2394 concerning sex education in public schools. It is our position that teaching that monogamous, heterosexual intercourse within marriage is a traditional American value is an unconstitutional establishment of religious doctrine in public schools. . . . We believe SB 2394 violates the First Amendment.

Again I stress, to me the question is not why modern secularists reject traditional morality, but on what grounds they defend any morality. Our legal system vigorously defends a woman's right to choose abortion—but why stop there? Historically, abandonment has been the more common means of disposing of unwanted children. Romans did it, Greeks did it, and during [philosopher Jean-Jacques] Rousseau's lifetime, one-third of babies in Paris were simply abandoned. Yet today in the United States, if a mother leaves her baby in a Chicago alley, or two teens deposit their newborn in a Dempsey Dumpster, they are subject to prosecution.

We feel outrage when we hear of a middle-class couple "dumping" an Alzheimer's-afflicted parent when they no longer wish to care for him, or when kids push a five-year-old out the window of a high-rise building, or a ten-year-old is raped in a hallway, or a mother drowns her two children because they interfere with her lifestyle. Why? On what grounds do we feel outrage if we truly believe that morality is self-determined? Evidently the people who committed the crimes felt no compunction. And if morality is not, in the end, self-determined, who determines it? On what basis do we decide?

In the landmark book *Faith in the Future*, Jonathan Sacks, chief rabbi of the United Hebrew Congregations of the (British) Commonwealth, argues that human society was meant to be a covenant between God and humankind, a collaborative enterprise based on common values and vision. Instead, it has become "an aggregate of individuals pursuing private interest, coming together temporarily and contractually, and leaving the state to resolve their conflicts on value-neutral grounds." In the process, "the individual loses his moorings . . . and becomes prone to a sense of meaninglessness and despair." Sacks argues that only by restoring the "moral covenant" can we reverse the breakdown in the social fabric of Western civilization.

Or, as the Jewish medical educator David C. Stolinsky put it, "The reason we fear to go out after dark is not that we may be set upon by bands of evangelicals and forced to read the New Testament, but that we may be set upon by gangs of feral young people who have been taught that nothing is superior to their own needs or feelings." . . .

In his study *Morality: Religious and Secular*, Basil Mitchell argues that since the eighteenth century, secular thinkers have attempted to make reason, not religion, the basis of morality. None has successfully found a way to establish an *absolute* value for the individual human person. Mitchell suggests that secular thinkers can establish a relative value for people, by comparing people to animals, say, or to each other; but the idea that every person has an absolute value came out of Christianity and Judaism before it and is absent from every other ancient philosophy or religion.

The Founding Fathers of the United States, apparently aware of the danger, made a valiant attempt to connect individual rights to a transcendent source. Overruling Thomas Jefferson, who had made only a vague reference to "the Laws of Nature and of Nature's God," they insisted instead on including the words "unalienable" and "endowed by their Creator." They did so in order to secure such rights in a transcendent Higher Power, so that no human power could attempt to take them away. Human dignity and worth derive from God's.

Yet if there is no Creator to endow these rights, on what basis can they be considered unalienable? Precisely that question is asked openly today. Robert Jarvik, a scientist and inventor of the artificial human heart, expresses the more modern view:

> In reality, there are no basic human rights. Mankind created them. They are conventions we agree to abide by for our mutual protection under law. Are there basic animal rights? Basic plant rights? Basic rights of any kind to protect things on our planet when the sun eventually burns out, or when we block it out with radioactive clouds? Someday, humans will realize that we are a part of nature and not separate from it. We have no more basic rights than viruses, other than those that we create for ourselves through our intellect and our compassion.

Jarvik captures the dilemma: If humans are not made in the image of God, somehow distinct from animals, what gives us any more rights than other species? Some animal rights activists already ask that question, and a writer in the journal *Wild Earth* even mused about the logical consequences:

> If you haven't given voluntary human extinction much thought before, the idea of a world with no people may seem strange. But, if you give the idea a chance I think you might agree that the extinction of *Homo sapiens* would mean survival for millions, if not billions, of other Earth-dwelling species.... Phasing out the human race will solve every problem on earth, social and environmental.

When representatives from the United States meet with their counterparts from China and Singapore to hammer out an agreement on human rights, not only do they have no common ground, they have no self-coherent ground on which to stand. Our founders made human dignity an irreducible value rooted in creation, a dignity that exists prior to any "public" status as citizen. Eliminate the Creator, and everything is on the negotiating table. By destroying the link between the social and cosmic orders, we have effectively destroyed the validity of the social order.

"Our ethics can be based neither upon fictions concerning the nature of mankind nor upon fake reports concerning the desire of the deities."

Morality Does Not Require Religious Belief

Frank R. Zindler

Contrary to common belief, religion is not the foundation of morality, writes Frank R. Zindler in the following viewpoint. Moral behavior is rooted in human physiology, inherited traits, and cultural adaptations, he maintains. What we consider to be ethical conduct is actually behavior that has, over time, proved to be of benefit to individuals and society. According to Zindler, religion is a cultural adaptation that was useful earlier in human evolution, but should now be replaced with scientific self-knowledge. He concludes that enlightened self-interest is more appropriate than religion as a modern moral compass. Zindler, a former professor of biology and geology, is managing editor of American Atheist *magazine.*

Frank R. Zindler, "Ethics Without Gods," *American Atheist*, February 1985. Reproduced by permission of the author.

As you read, consider the following questions:

1. What is the relationship between natural selection and morality, in Frank R. Zindler's opinion?

2. According to the author, what is cultural transmission?

3. How does Zindler define "enlightened self-interest"?

One of the first questions Atheists are asked by true believers and doubters alike is, "If you don't believe in a god, there's nothing to prevent you from committing crimes, is there? Without the fear of hell-fire and eternal damnation, you can do anything you like, can't you?"

It is hard to believe that even intelligent and educated people could hold such an opinion, but they do. It seems never to have occurred to them that the Greeks and Romans, whose gods and goddesses were something less than paragons of virtue, nevertheless led lives not obviously worse than those of the Baptists of Alabama. Moreover, pagans such as Aristotle and Marcus Aurelius—although their systems are not suitable for us today—managed to produce ethical treatises of great sophistication, a sophistication rarely, if ever, equaled by Christian moralists.

The answer to the question posed above is, of course, "Absolutely not!" The behavior of Atheists is subject to the same rules of sociology, psychology, and neurophysiology that govern the behavior of all members of our species, religionists included. Moreover, despite protestations to the contrary, we may assert as a general rule that when religionists practice ethical behavior, it isn't *really* due to their fear of hell-fire and damnation, or to their hopes of heaven. Ethical behavior—regardless of who the practitioner may be—results always from the same causes and is regulated by the same forces, and has nothing to do with the presence or absence of religious belief. The nature of these causes and forces is the subject of this essay.

Psychobiological Foundations

As human beings, we are social animals. Our sociality is the result of evolution, not choice. Natural selection has equipped us with nervous systems which are peculiarly sensitive to the emotional status of our fellows. Among our kind, emotions are contagious, and it is only the rare psychopathic mutants among us who can be happy in the midst of a sad society. It is in our nature to be happy in the midst of happiness, sad in the midst of sadness. It is in our nature, fortunately, to seek happiness for our fellows at the same time as we seek it for ourselves. Our happiness is greater when it is shared.

Nature also has provided us with nervous systems which are, to a considerable degree, imprintable. To be sure, this phenomenon is not as pronounced or as inelectable as it is, say, in geese—where a newly hatched gosling can be "imprinted" to a toy train and will follow it to exhaustion, as if it were its mother. Nevertheless, some degree of imprinting is exhibited by humans. The human nervous system appears to retain its capacity for imprinting well into old age, and it is highly likely that the phenomenon known as "love-at-first-sight" is a form of imprinting. Imprinting is a form of attachment behavior, and it helps us to form strong interpersonal bonds. It is a major force which helps us to break through the ego barrier to create "significant others" whom we can love as much as ourselves. These two characteristics of our nervous system—emotional suggestibility and attachment imprintability—although they are the foundation of all altruistic behavior and art, are thoroughly compatible with the selfishness characteristic of all behaviors created by the process of natural selection. That is to say, to a large extent behaviors which satisfy ourselves will be found simultaneously to satisfy our fellows and *vice-versa*.

This should not surprise us when we consider that among the societies of our nearest primate cousins, the great apes, social behavior is not chaotic, even if gorillas do lack the Ten

Commandments! The young chimpanzee does not need an oracle to tell it to honor its mother and to refrain from killing its brothers and sisters. Of course, family squabbles and even murder have been observed in ape societies, but such behaviors are exceptions, not the norm. So too it is in human societies, everywhere and at all times.

The African apes—whose genes are ninety-eight to ninety-nine percent identical to ours—go about their lives as social animals, cooperating in the living of life, entirely without the benefit of clergy and without the commandments of Exodus, Leviticus, or Deuteronomy. It is further cheering to learn that sociobiologists have even observed altruistic behavior among troops of baboons! More than once, in troops attacked by leopards, aged, post-reproduction-age males have been observed to linger at the rear of the escaping troop and to engage the leopard in what often amounts to a suicidal fight. As an old male delays the leopard's pursuit by sacrificing his very life, the females and young escape and live to fulfill their several destinies. The heroism which we see acted out, from time to time, by our fellow men and women, is far older than their religions. Long before the gods were created by the fear-filled minds of our less courageous ancestors, heroism and acts of self-sacrificing love existed. They did not require a supernatural excuse, then, nor do they require one now.

Given the general fact, then, that evolution has equipped us with nervous systems biased in favor of social, rather than antisocial, behaviors, is it not true, nevertheless, that antisocial behavior *does* exist? And does it not exist in amounts greater than a reasonable ethicist would find tolerable? Alas, this is true. But is true largely because we live in worlds far more complex than the Paleolithic world in which our nervous systems originated. To understand the ethical significance of this fact, we must digress a bit and review the evolutionary history of human behavior.

Instinctual and Learned Behavior

Today, heredity can control our behavior in only the most general of ways; it cannot dictate precise behaviors appropriate for infinitely varied circumstances. In our world, heredity needs help.

In the world of a fruit fly, by contrast, the problems to be solved are few in number and highly predictable in nature. Consequently, a fruit fly's brain is largely "hard-wired" by heredity. That is to say, most behaviors result from environmental activation of nerve circuits which are formed automatically by the time of emergence of the adult fly. This is an extreme example of what is called instinctual behavior. Each behavior is coded for by a gene or genes which predispose the nervous system to develop certain types of circuits and not others, and it is all but impossible to act contrary to the genetically predetermined script.

The world of a mammal—say a fox—is much more complex and unpredictable than that of the fruit fly. Consequently, a fox is born with only a portion of its neuronal circuitry hard-wired. Many of its neurons remain "plastic" throughout life. That is, they may or may not hook up with each other in functional circuits, depending upon environmental circumstances. Learned behavior is behavior which results from activation of these environmentally conditioned circuits. Learning allows the individual mammal to assimilate—by trial and error—greater numbers of adaptive behaviors than could be transmitted by heredity. A fox would be wall-to-wall genes if all its behaviors were specified genetically!

With the evolution of humans, however, environmental complexity increased out of all proportion to the genetic and neuronal changes distinguishing us from our simian ancestors. This was due partly to the fact that our species evolved in a geologic period of great climatic flux—the Ice Ages—and partly to the fact that our behaviors themselves began to change our environment. The changed environment in turn created new problems to be solved. Their solutions further changed the environment, and so on. Thus, the discovery of fire led to the burning of trees and forests, which led to destruction of local water supplies and watersheds, which led to the development of architecture with which to build aqueducts, which led to laws concerning water rights, which led to international strife, and on and on.

Given such complexity, even the ability to learn new behaviors is, by itself, inadequate. If trial and error were the only means, most people would die of old age before they would succeed in rediscovering fire or reinventing the wheel. As a substitute for instinct and to increase the efficiency of learning, mankind developed culture. The ability to teach—as well as to learn—evolved, and trial-and-error learning became a method of last resort.

By transmission of culture—passing on the sum total of the learned behaviors common to a population—we can do what Darwinian genetic selection would not allow: We can inherit acquired characteristics. The wheel once having been invented, its manufacture and use can be passed down through generations. Culture can adapt to change much faster than genes can, and this provides for finely tuned responses to environmental disturbances and upheavals. By means of cultural transmission, those behaviors which have proven useful in the past can be taught quickly to the young, so that adaptation to life—say on the Greenland ice cap—can be assured.

Even so, cultural transmission tends to be rigid: It took over one hundred thousand years to advance to chipping *both* sides of the hand ax! Cultural mutations, like genetic mutations, tend more often than not to be harmful, and both are resisted—the former by cultural conservatism, the latter by natural selection. But changes do creep in faster than the rate of genetic change, and cultures slowly evolve. Even that cultural dinosaur known as the Roman Catholic church—despite its claim to be the unchanging repository of truth and correct behavior—has changed greatly since its beginning.

Incidentally, it is this hand ax stage of behavioral evolution at which most of the religions of today are still stuck. Our inflexible, absolutist moral codes also are fixated at this stage. The Ten Commandments are the moral counterpart of the "here's-how-you-rub-the-sticks-together" phase of technological evolution. If the only type of fire you want is one to heat your cave and cook your clams, the stick-rubbing method suffices. But if you want a fire to propel your jet airplane, some changes have to be made.

So, too, with the transmission of moral behavior. If we are to live lives which are as complex socially as jet airplanes are complex technologically, we need something more than the Ten Commandments. We cannot base our moral code upon arbitrary and capricious fiats reported to us by persons claiming to be privy to the intentions of the denizens of Sinai or Olympus. Our ethics can be based neither upon fictions concerning the nature of mankind nor upon fake reports concerning the desire of the deities. Our ethics must be firmly planted in the soil of scientific self-knowledge. They must be *improvable* and *adaptable*.

Where then, and with what, shall we begin?

The Principle of Enlightened Self-Interest

The principle of "enlightened self-interest" is an excellent first approximation to an ethical principle which is both consistent with what we know of human nature and is relevant to the problems of life in a complex society. Let us examine this principle.

First we must distinguish between "enlightened" and "unenlightened" self-interest. Let's take an extreme example for illustration. Suppose a person lived a totally selfish life of immediate gratification of every desire. Suppose that whenever someone else had something he wanted, he took it for himself.

It wouldn't be long at all before everyone would be up in arms against him, and he would have to spend all his waking hours fending off reprisals. Depending upon how outrageous his activity had been, he might very well lose his life in an orgy of neighborly revenge. The life of total but unenlightened self-interest might be exciting and pleasant as long as it lasts—but it is not likely to last long.

The person who practices "enlightened" self-interest, by contrast, is the person whose behavioral strategy simultaneously maximizes both the *intensity* and *duration* of personal gratification. An enlightened strategy will be one which, when practiced over a long span of time, will generate ever greater amounts and varieties of pleasures and satisfactions.

How is this to be done?

It is obvious that more is to be gained by cooperating with others than by acts of isolated egoism. One man with a rock cannot kill a buffalo for dinner. But a group of men or women, with a lot of rocks, can drive the beast off a cliff and—even after dividing the meat up among them—will still have more to eat than they would have had without cooperation.

Cooperation

But cooperation is a two-way street. If you cooperate with several others to kill buffalo, and each time they drive you away from the kill and eat it themselves, you will quickly take your services elsewhere, and you will leave the ingrates to stumble along without the Paleolithic equivalent of a fourth-for-bridge. Cooperation implies reciprocity.

Justice has its roots in the problem of determining fairness and reciprocity in cooperation. If I cooperate with you in tilling your field of corn, how much of the corn is due me at harvest time? When there is justice, cooperation operates at maximal efficiency, and the fruits of cooperation become ever more desirable. Thus, "enlightened self-interest" entails a desire for justice. With justice and with cooperation, we can have symphonies. Without it, we haven't even a song.

Because we have the nervous systems of social animals, we are generally happier in the company of our fellow creatures than alone. Because we are emotionally suggestible, as we practice enlightened self-interest, we usually will be wise to choose behaviors which will make others happy and willing to cooperate and accept us—for their happiness will reflect back upon us and intensify our own happiness. On the other hand, actions which harm others and make them unhappy—even if they do not trigger overt retaliation which decreases our happiness—will create an emotional milieu, which because of our suggestibility, will make us less happy.

Because our nervous systems are imprintable, we are able not only to fall in love at first sight, we are able to love objects and ideals as well as people. We are also able to love with variable intensities. Like the gosling attracted to the toy train, we are pulled forward by the desire for love. Unlike the gosling's "love," however, our love is to a considerable extent shapable by experience and is educable. A major aim of "enlightened self-interest," surely, is to give and receive love, both sexual and non-sexual. As a general—though not absolute—rule, we must choose those behaviors which will be likely to bring us love and acceptance, and we must eschew those behaviors which will not.

Another aim of enlightened self-interest is to seek beauty in all its forms, to preserve and prolong its resonance between the world outside and that within. Beauty and love are but different facets of the same jewel: Love is beautiful, and we love beauty.

The experience of love and beauty, however, is a *passive* function of the mind. How much greater is the joy which comes from creating beauty! How delicious it is to exercise *ac-*

tively our creative powers to engender that which can be loved! Paints and pianos are not necessarily prerequisites for the exercise of creativity. Whenever one transforms the raw materials of existence in such a way that he leaves them better than they were when he found them, he has been creative.

The Task of Moral Education

The task of moral education, then, is not to inculcate by rote great lists of do's and don'ts but rather to help people to predict the consequences of actions being considered. What are the long-term and immediate rewards and drawbacks of the acts? Will an act increase or decrease one's chances of experiencing the hedonic triad of love, beauty, and creativity?

Thus it happens, that when the Atheist approaches the problem of finding natural grounds for human morals and establishing a non-superstitious basis for behavior, it appears as though nature has already solved the problem to a great extent. Indeed, it appears as though the problem of establishing a natural, humanistic basis for ethical behavior is not much of a problem at all. It is in our natures to desire love, to seek beauty, and to thrill at the act of creation. The labyrinthine complexity we see when we examine traditional moral codes does not arise of necessity: It is largely the result of vain attempts to accommodate human needs and nature to the whimsical totems and taboos of the demons and deities who emerged with us from our cave dwellings at the end of the Paleolithic Era—and have haunted our houses ever since.

"[Secular humanists] wish to encourage wherever possible the growth of moral awareness and the capacity for free choice."

Secular Humanism Encourages Moral Awareness

Paul Kurtz

Paul Kurtz is founder and chair of the Council for Secular Humanism and president of the International Academy of Humanism. He is also editor in chief of Free Inquiry, *a quarterly journal of humanist thought. In the following viewpoint, Kurtz defines some of the principles of secular humanism, a worldview that upholds reason, freedom, and human rights while opposing religious belief and superstition. Kurtz maintains that secular humanism has greatly contributed to the development of a more humane and democratic world. By promoting freedom of thought, church-state separation, and systems of ethics informed by reason, secular humanism provides a way for people to articulate moral principles.*

Paul Kurtz, "A Secular Humanist Declaration," The Council for Secular Humanism, 1980. Reproduced by permission.

As you read, consider the following questions:

1. What antisecularist trends does the world face today, in Paul Kurtz's opinion?

2. According to the author, who are some secularists and humanists who have demonstrated morality in their lives and works?

3. According to Kurtz, why do secularists believe it is immoral to baptize infants or confirm adolescents?

Secular humanism is a vital force in the contemporary world. It is now under unwarranted and intemperate attack from various quarters. This declaration defends only that form of secular humanism which is explicitly committed to democracy. It is opposed to all varieties of belief that seek supernatural sanction for their values or espouse rule by dictatorship.

Democratic secular humanism has been a powerful force in world culture. Its ideals can be traced to the philosophers, scientists, and poets of classical Greece and Rome, to ancient Chinese Confucian society, to the Carvaka movement of India, and to other distinguished intellectual and moral traditions. Secularism and humanism were eclipsed in Europe during the Dark Ages, when religious piety eroded humankind's confidence in its own powers to solve human problems. They reappeared in force during the Renaissance with the reassertion of secular and humanist values in literature and the arts, again in the sixteenth and seventeenth centuries with the development of modern science and a naturalistic view of the universe, and their influence can be found in eighteenth century in the Age of Reason and the Enlightenment.

Democratic secular humanism has creatively flowered in modern times with the growth of freedom and democracy. Countless millions of thoughtful persons have espoused secular humanist ideals, have lived significant lives, and have contributed to the building of a more humane and democratic world. The modern secular humanist outlook has led to the application of science and technology to the improvement of the human condition. This has had a positive effect on reducing poverty, suffering, and disease in various parts of the world, in extending longevity, on improving transportation and communication, and in making the good life possible for more and more people. It has led to the emancipation of hundreds of millions of people from the exercise of blind faith and fears of superstition and has contributed to their education and the enrichment of their lives.

Antisecularist Trends

Secular humanism has provided an impetus for humans to solve their problems with intelligence and perseverance, to conquer geographic and social frontiers, and to extend the range of human exploration and adventure. Regrettably, we are today faced with a variety of antisecularist trends: the reappearance of dogmatic authoritarian religions; fundamentalist, literalist, and doctrinaire Christianity; a rapidly growing and uncompromising Moslem clericalism in the Middle East and Asia; the reassertion of orthodox authority by the Roman Catholic papal hierarchy; nationalistic religious Judaism; and the reversion to obscurantist religions in Asia.

New cults of unreason as well as bizarre paranormal and occult beliefs, such as belief in astrology, reincarnation, and the mysterious power of alleged psychics, are growing in many Western societies. These disturbing developments follow in the wake of the emergence in the earlier part of the twentieth century of intolerant messianic and totalitarian quasi religious movements, such as fascism and communism. These religious activists not only are responsible for much of the terror and violence in the world today but stand in the way of solutions to the world's most serious problems.

Paradoxically, some of the critics of secular humanism maintain that it is a dangerous philosophy. Some assert that it is "morally corrupting" because it is committed to individual freedom, others that it condones "injustice" because it defends democratic due process. We who support democratic secular humanism deny such charges, which are based upon misunderstanding and misinterpretation, and we seek to outline a set of principles that most of us share.

Secular humanism is not a dogma or a creed. There are wide differences of opinion among secular humanists on many issues. Nevertheless, there is a loose consensus with respect to several propositions. We are apprehensive that modern civilization is threatened by forces antithetical to reason, democracy, and freedom. Many religious believers will no doubt share with us a belief in many secular humanist and democratic values, and we welcome their joining with us in the defense of these ideals.

Free Inquiry

The first principle of democratic secular humanism is its commitment to free inquiry. We oppose any tyranny over the mind of man, any efforts by ecclesiastical, political, ideological, or social institutions to shackle free thought. In the past, such tyrannies have been directed by churches and states attempting to enforce the edicts of religious bigots. In the long struggle in the history of ideas, established institutions, both public and private, have attempted to censor inquiry, to impose orthodoxy on beliefs and values, and to excommunicate heretics and extirpate unbelievers. Today, the struggle for free inquiry has assumed new forms. Sectarian ideologies have become the new theologies that use political parties and governments in their mission to crush dissident opinion. Free inquiry entails recognition of civil liberties as integral to its pursuit, that is, a free press, freedom of communication, the right to organize opposition parties and to join voluntary as-

What the Humanist Believes

Humanism is opposed to all theories of universal determinism, fatalism, or predestination and believes that human beings possess genuine freedom of choice (free will) in making decisions both important and unimportant. Free choice is conditioned by inheritance, education, the external environment (including economic conditions), and other factors. Nonetheless, it remains real and substantial. Humanism rejects both Marxist economic determinism and Christian theistic determinism.

Humanism advocates an ethics or morality that grounds all human values in this-earthly experiences and relationships, and that views man as a functioning unity of physical, emotional, and intellectual faculties. The humanist holds as his highest ethical goal the this-worldly happiness, freedom, and progress—economic, cultural, and material—of all mankind, irrespective of nation, race, religion, sex, or economic status. Reserving the word *love* for their families and friends, he has an attitude of *compassionate concern* toward his fellow men in general.

Corliss Lamont, Humanist, *September/October 1971*.

sociations, and freedom to cultivate and publish the fruits of scientific, philosophical, artistic, literary, moral and religious freedom. Free inquiry requires that we tolerate diversity of opinion and that we respect the right of individuals to express their beliefs, however unpopular they may be, without social or legal prohibition or fear of sanctions. Though we may tolerate contrasting points of view, this does not mean that they are immune to critical scrutiny. The guiding premise of those who believe in free inquiry is that truth is more likely to be discovered if the opportunity exists for the free exchange of opposing opinions; the process of interchange is frequently as important as the result. This applies not only to science and to everyday life, but to politics, economics, morality, and religion.

Separation of Church and State

Because of their commitment to freedom, secular humanists believe in the principle of the separation of church and state. The lessons of history are clear: Wherever one religion or ideology is established and given a dominant position in the state, minority opinions are in jeopardy. A pluralistic, open, democratic society allows all points of view to be heard. Any effort to impose an exclusive conception of Truth, Piety, Virtue, or Justice upon the whole of society is a violation of free inquiry. Clerical authorities should not be permitted to legislate their own parochial views—whether moral, philosophical, political, educational, or social—for the rest of society. Nor should tax revenues be exacted for the benefit or support of sectarian religious institutions. Individuals and voluntary associations should be free to accept or not to accept any belief and to support these convictions with whatever resources they may have, without being compelled by taxation to contribute to those religious faiths with which they do not agree. . . .

Ethics Based on Critical Intelligence

The moral views of secular humanism have been subjected to criticism by religious fundamentalist theists. The secular humanist recognizes the central role of morality in human life; indeed, ethics was developed as a branch of human knowledge long before religionists proclaimed their moral systems based upon divine authority. The field of ethics has had a distinguished list of thinkers contributing to its development: from Socrates, Democritus, Aristotle, Epicurus, and Epictetus, to Spinoza, Erasmus, Hume, Voltaire, Kant, Bentham, Mill, G.E. Moore, Bertrand Russell, John Dewey, and others. There is an influential philosophical tradition that maintains that ethics is an autonomous field of inquiry, that ethical judgments can be formulated independently of revealed religion, and that human beings can cultivate practical reason and wisdom and, by its application, achieve lives of virtue and excellence. Moreover, philosophers have emphasized the need to cultivate an appreciation for the requirements of social justice and for an individual's obligations and responsibilities toward others. Thus, secularists deny that morality needs to be deduced from religious belief or that those who do not espouse a religious doctrine are immoral. For secular humanists, ethical conduct is, or should be, judged by critical reason, and their goal is to develop autonomous and responsible individuals, capable of making their own choices in life based upon an understanding of human behavior. Morality that is not God-based need not be antisocial, subjective, or promiscuous, nor need it lead to the breakdown of moral standards. Although we believe in tolerating diverse lifestyles and social manners, we do not think they are immune to criticism. Nor do we believe that any one church should impose its views of moral virtue and sin, sexual conduct, marriage, divorce, birth control, or abortion, or legislate them for the rest of society. As secular humanists we believe in the central importance of the value of human happiness here and now. We are opposed to absolutist morality, yet we maintain that objective standards emerge, and ethical values and principles may be discovered, in the course of ethical deliberation. Secular humanist ethics maintains that it is possible for human beings to lead meaningful and wholesome lives for themselves and in service to their fellow human beings without the need of religious commandments or the benefit of clergy. There have been any number of distinguished secularists and humanists who have demonstrated moral principles in their personal lives and works: Protagoras, Lucretius, Epicurus, Spinoza, Hume, Thomas Paine, Diderot, Mark Twain, George Eliot, John Stuart Mill, Ernest Renan, Charles

Darwin, Thomas Edison, Clarence Darrow, Robert Ingersoll, Gilbert Murray, Albert Schweitzer, Albert Einstein, Max Born, Margaret Sanger, and Bertrand Russell, among others.

We believe that moral development should be cultivated in children and young adults. We do not believe that any particular sect can claim important values as their exclusive property; hence it is the duty of public education to deal with these values. Accordingly, we support moral education in the schools that is designed to develop an appreciation for moral virtues, intelligence, and the building of character. We wish to encourage wherever possible the growth of moral awareness and the capacity for free choice and an understanding of the consequences thereof. We do not think it is moral to baptize infants, to confirm adolescents, or to impose a religious creed on young people before they are able to consent. Although children should learn about the history of religious moral practices, these young minds should not be indoctrinated in a faith before they are mature enough to evaluate the merits for themselves. It should be noted that secular humanism is not so much a specific morality as it is a method for the explanation and discovery of rational moral principles. . . .

Religious Skepticism

Religions are pervasive sociological phenomena, and religious myths have long persisted in human history. In spite of the fact that human beings have found religions to be uplifting and a source of solace, we do not find their theological claims to be true. Religions have made negative as well as positive contributions toward the development of human civilization. Although they have helped to build hospitals and schools and, at their best, have encouraged the spirit of love and charity, many have also caused human suffering by being intolerant of those who did not accept their dogmas or creeds. Some religions have been fanatical and repressive, narrowing human hopes, limiting aspirations, and precipitating religious wars and violence. While religions have no doubt offered comfort to the bereaved and dying by holding forth the promise of an immortal life, they have also aroused morbid fear and dread. We have found no convincing evidence that there is a separable "soul" or that it exists before birth or survives death. We must therefore conclude that the ethical life can be lived without the illusions of immortality or reincarnation. Human beings can develop the self confidence necessary to ameliorate the human condition and to lead meaningful, productive lives. . . .

Approaching the Human Situation Realistically

Democratic secular humanism is too important for human civilization to abandon. Reasonable persons will surely recognize its profound contributions to human welfare. We are nevertheless surrounded by doomsday prophets of disaster, always wishing to turn the clock back—they are anti science, anti freedom, anti human. In contrast, the secular humanistic outlook is basically melioristic, looking forward with hope rather than backward with despair. We are committed to extending the ideals of reason, freedom, individual and collective opportunity, and democracy throughout the world community. The problems that humankind will face in the future, as in the past, will no doubt be complex and difficult. However, if it is to prevail, it can only do so by enlisting resourcefulness and courage. Secular humanism places trust in human intelligence rather than in divine guidance. Skeptical of theories of redemption, damnation, and reincarnation, secular humanists attempt to approach the human situation in realistic terms: Human beings are responsible for their own destinies. We believe that it is possible to bring about a more humane world, one based upon the methods of reason and the principles of tolerance, compromise, and the negotiations of difference.

> "Secular societies believe they have left religion behind, when all they have done is substitute one set of myths for another."

Secular Humanism Is Harmful

John Gray

In the following viewpoint, John Gray argues that secular humanism is harmful because it suppresses natural human inclinations and fosters tyranny in the name of progress and science. Liberal humanism is actually a secular cult that developed out of Christianity's separation of religion and politics. In effect, Gray explains, secular humanism is a belief system that tries to deny its own religious roots. What secularists fail to recognize is that religious belief is a natural human impulse, Gray contends. When secular societies attempt to deny religion, the repressed religious instinct eventually reasserts itself in bizarre and dangerous ways. Gray is the author of many books on political theory and a professor of European thought at the London School of Economics in England.

John Gray, "The Myth of Secularism: Religion Is a Natural Human Impulse, Which Our Society Tries to Repress Just as the Victorians Did Sex. That Is Why Atheists Are So Rancorous and Intolerant," *New Statesman*, vol. 131, December 16, 2002, pp. 69–71. Copyright © 2002 by New Statesman, Ltd. Reproduced by permission.

As you read, consider the following questions:

1. According to John Gray, what is the biblical root of the secular state?

2. What is positivism, according to the author?

3. In what way are Christian myths more realistic than secular doctrines, in Gray's opinion?

Of all the myths spawned by the Enlightenment, the idea that we live in a secular age is the most absurd. Throughout much of the world, religion is thriving with undiminished vitality. Where believers are in the minority, as they are in Britain today, traditional faiths have been replaced by liberal humanism, which is now established as the unthinking creed of conventional people. Yet liberal humanism is itself very obviously a religion—a shoddy derivative of Christian faith notably more irrational than the original article, and in recent times more harmful. If this is not recognised, it is because religion has been repressed from consciousness in the way that sexuality was repressed in Victorian times. Now as then, the result is not that the need disappears, but rather that it returns in bizarre and perverse forms. Secular societies may imagine they are post-religious, but actually they are ruled by repressed religion.

When thinking about the idea that we live in a post-religious era, it is worth remembering that the secular realm is a Christian invention. The biblical root of the secular state is the passage in the New Testament where Jesus tells his disciples to give to God what is God's and to Caesar what belongs to Caesar. Refined by Augustine and given a modern formulation with the Reformation, this early Christian commandment is the ultimate origin of the liberal attempt to separate religion from politics. In this, as in many other respects, liberalism is a neo-Christian cult.

Liberalism's Religious Roots

Liberalism's religious roots are opaque to liberals today, but a little history makes them clear. In Britain, until the late 19th century, most liberals were believers. It was churchmen who most consistently upheld causes such as the abolition of slavery; the more radical thinkers belonged to fringe Christian denominations such as the Quakers and the Unitarians. Only with John Stuart Mill, when he came under the influence of the French positivist thinker Auguste Comte, did liberalism come to be closely associated with outright rejection of conventional religion. Positivism is largely forgotten today, and not without good reason. Nevertheless, it was more influential than any other intellectual movement in shaping the humanist creed that has succeeded Christianity as the ready-made worldview of the British majority. The positivists were not liberals—far from it. They aimed to found a new religion—the Religion of Humanity, as they called it—in which the human species would be worshipped as the supreme being, and they looked forward to a time when this new religion would have as much power as the Catholic Church had in mediaeval times. They were eager to emulate the Church's rituals and hierarchies. They sought to replace the Catholic practice of crossing oneself by a secular version, in which positivist believers touched the bumps on their heads at the points where the science of phrenology had shown the impulses of order and benevolence to reside. They also installed a secular pope in Paris. In its early 19th-century heyday, the Positivist Church had Temples of Humanity in many parts of the world, including Britain. It was particularly successful in Latin America, where a number of positivist churches survive to this day.

The Positivist Church was a travesty, but its beliefs chimed with many of Mill's. Though he attacked Comte's anti-liberal tendencies, Mill did everything he could to propagate the Religion of Humanity. If he had some success, the reason was chiefly that the new humanist religion had a great deal in common with the creed it was meant to supplant. Liberal humanism inherits several key Christian beliefs—above all, the belief that humans are categorically different from all other animals. According to humanists, humans are unique in that, using the power over nature given them by science, they can create a world better than any that has existed before. In this view, the earth is simply a mass of resources for human use, and the other animals with which we share it have no value in themselves. Those who hold to this view of things see themselves as tough-minded scientific realists, but in fact they are in the grip of one of the worst legacies of Christianity. The humanist view of the earth as an instrument of human purpose is a secular rendition of the biblical myth of Genesis. . . .

The Trouble with Secular Myths

The role of hollowed-out versions of Christian myth in humanist thought is particularly clear in the case of Marxism. Marx's absurd idea of "the end of history", in which communism triumphs and destructive conflict then vanishes from the world, is transparently a secular mutation of Christian apocalyptic beliefs. The same is true of Francis Fukuyama's equally preposterous belief in universal salvation through "global democratic capitalism". In both cases, what we have is myth masquerading as science.

The trouble with secular myths is that they are frequently more harmful than the real thing. In traditional Christianity, the apocalyptic impulse was restrained by the insight that human beings are ineradicably flawed. In the secular religions that flowed from Christianity, this insight was lost. The result has been a form of tyranny, new in history, that commits vast crimes in the pursuit of heaven on earth.

Atheist Regimes

The role of humanist thought in shaping the past century's worst regimes is easily demonstrable, but it is passed over, or denied, by those who harp on about the crimes of religion. Yet the mass murders of the 20th century were not perpetrated by some latter-day version of the Spanish Inquisition. They were done by atheist regimes in the service of Enlightenment ideals of progress. Stalin and Mao were not believers in original sin. Even Hitler, who despised Enlightenment values of equality and freedom, shared the Enlightenment faith that a new world could be created by human will. Each of these tyrants imagined that the human condition could be transformed through the use of science.

History has demolished these ambitions. Even so, they have not been abandoned. In dilute and timorous forms, they continue to animate liberal humanists. Humanists angrily deny harbouring the vast hopes of Marx or Comte, but still insist that the growth of scientific knowledge enables mankind to construct a future better than anything in the past. There is not the slightest scientific warrant for this belief. It is faith, pure and simple. More, it is Christian faith—the myth that, unlike other animals, "we" can shape the future.

The irony of secular cultures is that they are ruled by myths. It is a commonplace that science has displaced religion. What is less often noted is that science has become a vehicle for needs that are indisputably religious. Like religion in the past, though less effectively, science offers meaning and hope. In politics, improvement is fragmentary and reversible. In science, the growth of knowledge is cumulative and now seemingly unstoppable. Science gives a sensation of progress that politics cannot deliver. It is an illusion, but that in no way diminishes its power. We may live in a post-Christian culture, but the idea of providence has not disappeared. People still need to believe that a benign pattern can be glimpsed in the chaos of human events.

The Repression of Religious Experience

The need for religion appears to be hard-wired in the human animal. Certainly the behaviour of secular humanists supports this hypothesis. Atheists are usually just as emotionally engaged as believers. Quite commonly, they are more intellectually rigid. One cannot engage in dialogue with religious thinkers in Britain today without quickly discovering that they are, on the whole, more intelligent, better educated and strikingly more freethinking than unbelievers (as evangelical atheists still incongruously describe themselves). No doubt there are many reasons for this state of affairs, but I suspect it is the repression of the religious impulse that explains the obsessive rigidity of secular thought.

Liberal humanists repress religious experience—in themselves and others—in much the way that sexuality was repressed in the strait-laced societies of the past. When I refer to repression here, I mean it in precisely the Freudian sense. In secular cultures, religion is buried in the unconscious, only to reappear—as sex did among the Victorians—in grotesque and illicit forms. If, as some claim, the Victorians covered piano legs in a vain effort to exorcise sex from their lives, secular humanists behave similarly when they condemn religion as irrational. It seems not to have occurred to them to ask where it comes from. History and anthropology show it to be a species-wide phenomenon. There is no more reason to think that we will cease to be religious animals than there is to think we will someday be asexual.

Whatever their disciples may say today, Karl Marx and John Stuart Mill were adamant that religion would die out with the advance of science. That has not come about, and there is not the remotest prospect of it happening in the foreseeable future. Yet the idea that religion can be eradicated from human life remains an anxiously defended article of faith among secular humanists. As secular ideology is dumped throughout the world, they are left disoriented and gawping.

A Basic Need

Most of the people I met in intellectual, academic, or liberal circles seemed to feel that religion and spirituality were for people who were culturally or intellectually retarded, for people who couldn't handle the world and hence "needed that sort of thing." The very idea of "needing" was seen as a sign of being weak, undeveloped, retarded, because, of course, people who are cool can stand alone without "need" of anything or anyone. It was these "ordinary people," I was taught, who were such jerks that they . . . clung to religion and spirituality because thinking in a clear and rational way was beyond their capacities and scared them too much. . . .

But what I discovered was something quite different, namely, that [ordinary people] . . . were just as concerned with meaning as anyone else, including any of us who consider ourselves intellectual or agents of social change.

Connection to Spirit is as essential as oxygen. It's a basic need.

Yet, we have taught ourselves to see people as a bunch of isolated machines driven by the need for food, sex, and power. We have acted as though we could cut ourselves off from our Divine essence as manifestations of Spirit. We have built social and economic institutions and have raised children as though we did not know that we are part of the spiritual order of the universe and that our hunger for spiritual connection is every bit as urgent as our hunger for food.

Michael Lerner, Spirit Matters, *2000.*

It is this painful cognitive dissonance, I believe, that accounts for the peculiar rancour and intolerance of many secular thinkers. Unable to account for the irrepressible vitality of religion, they can react only with puritanical horror and stigmatise it as irrational. Yet the truth is that if religion is irrational, so is the human animal. As is shown by the behavior of humanists, this is never more so than when it imagines itself to be ruled by reason. . . .

The Paradox of Secularism

Here we have the paradox of secularism. Secular societies believe they have left religion behind, when all they have done is substitute one set of myths for another. It is far from clear that this amounts to an improvement. Christian myth has harmful aspects, not least its ingrained anthropocentrism. Even so, in insisting that human nature is incorrigibly flawed it is far more realistic than the secular doctrines that followed it. In effect, liberal humanism has taken Christianity's unhappiest myth—the separation of humans from the rest of the natural world—and stripped it of the transcendental content that gave it meaning. In so doing, it has left secular cultures such as Britain stuck between a humanist view of mankind that actually comes from religion and a more genuinely scientific view in which it is just one animal species, no more capable of taking charge of its destiny than any other. . . .

Humanism is not an alternative to religious belief, but rather a degenerate and unwitting version of it. Among the many varieties of religious life that are thriving among us—Hindu and Buddhist, Jewish and Muslim, along with many new and hybrid traditions—this pale shadow of Christianity is surely an anomaly.

Weighed down with fears and anxieties that the rest of us have never known or have long since left behind, it survives only as a remnant of a time when religion suppressed natural human impulses. We may not be far from a time when atheism will be seen as a relic of repression, like the frills that may once have been draped over piano legs.

"There is good evidence for the existence of genuine altruism."

Altruism Promotes Moral Behavior

Alfie Kohn

Alfie Kohn speaks and writes widely on human behavior, education, and parenting. He is the author of Punished by Rewards *and* No Contest: The Case Against Competition. *In the viewpoint that follows, Kohn maintains that helpful behavior is primarily motivated by altruism. While many philosophers and psychologists have argued that people generally act out of self-interest—even when they are apparently helping others—recent research suggests that those who voluntarily help are generally not seeking to impress others or ease their own feelings of distress. Instead, Kohn asserts, they are acting out of empathy—the ability to feel other people's pain and to understand other people's perspectives.*

As you read, consider the following questions:

1. What kind of people are most likely to assist others, according to Alfie Kohn?

Alfie Kohn, "Beyond Selfishness: We Start Helping Others Early in Life, but We're Not Always Consistent," *Psychology Today*, vol. 22, October 1988, pp. 34–37. Copyright © 1991–2007 Sussex Publishers LLC. Reproduced by permission.

2. What experiments have been conducted to define what motivates people to help others, according to the author?

3. In Kohn's view, how does culture influence our motivation to care about others?

You realize you left your wallet on the bus and you give up hope of ever seeing it again. But someone calls that evening asking how to return the wallet to you.

Two toddlers are roughhousing when one suddenly begins to cry. The other child rushes to fetch his own security blanket and offers it to his playmate.

Driving on a lonely country road, you see a car stopped on the shoulder, smoke pouring from the hood. The driver waves to you frantically, and instinctively you pull over to help, putting aside thoughts of your appointments.

Prosocial Behavior

Despite the fact that "Look out for Number One" is one of our culture's mantras, these examples of "prosocial" behavior are really not so unusual. "Even in our society," says New York University psychologist Martin Hoffman, "the evidence is overwhelming that most people, when confronted with someone in a distress situation, will make a move to help very quickly if circumstances permit."

Helping may be as dramatic as agreeing to donate a kidney or as mundane as letting another shopper ahead of you in line. But most of us do it frequently and started doing it very early in life.

Psychologists have argued for years about whether our behavior owes more to the situations in which we find ourselves or to our individual characteristics. Prosocial behavior seems to be related to both. On the situation side, research shows that regardless of your personality, you'll be more likely to come to someone's aid if that person is already known to you or is seen as similar to you. Likewise, if you live in a small town rather than a city, the chances of your agreeing to help increase dramatically. In one experiment, a child stood on a busy street and said to passersby, "I'm lost. Can you call my house?" Nearly three-quarters of the adults in small towns did so, as compared with fewer than half in big cities. "City people adjust to the constant demands of urban life by reducing their involvement with others," the researcher concluded. You are also more likely to help someone if no one else is around at the time you hear a cry for help. The original research on this question was conducted by psychologists Bibb Latané and John Darley. They offer three reasons to account for the fact that we're less apt to help when more people are in the area: First, we may get a case of stage fright, fearing to appear foolish if it turns out no help was really necessary. Second, we may conclude from the fact that other people aren't helping that there's really no need for us to intervene either. Finally, the responsibility for doing something is shared by everyone present, so we don't feel a personal obligation to get involved.

But some people seem to be more other-oriented than others regardless of the situation. People who feel in control of what happens in their lives and who have little need for approval from others are the most likely to help others. Similarly, people in a good state of mind, even if only temporarily, are especially inclined to help. "Feel good, do good" is the general rule, researchers say, regardless of whether you feel good from having had a productive day at the office or, say, from finding money in the street. In one study, people got a phone call from a woman who said the operator had given her their number by mistake, and she was now out of change at a pay phone. The woman asked if the person who answered would look up a number, call and deliver a message for her. It turned out that people who had unexpectedly received free stationery a few minutes before were more likely to help out the caller.

Motives for Helping Others

But some investigators aren't satisfied with knowing just when prosocial acts will take place or by whom. "Why should we help other people? Why not help Number One? That's the rock-bottom question," says University of Massachusetts psychologist Ervin Staub, who's been wrestling with that problem since the mid 1960s.

Obviously we do help each other. But it's equally obvious that our motives for doing so aren't always unselfish. Prosocial behavior, which means behavior intended to benefit others, isn't necessarily altruistic. The 17th-century political philosopher Thomas Hobbes, who believed that we always act out of self-interest, was once seen giving money to a beggar. When asked why, he explained that he was mostly trying to relieve his own distress at seeing the beggar's distress.

His explanation will ring true for many of us. But is this always what's going on: helping in order to feel good or to benefit ourselves in some way? Is real altruism a Sunday school myth? Many of us automatically assume so—not because there's good evidence for that belief but because of our basic, and unproved, assumptions about human nature.

Evidence of Genuine Altruism

New research describes how we feel when helping someone, but that doesn't mean we came to that person's aid in order to feel good. We may have acted out of a simple desire to help. In fact, there is good evidence for the existence of genuine altruism. Consider:

• Do we help just to impress others? "If looking good were the motive, you'd be more likely to help with others watching," says Latané. His experiments showed just the opposite. More evidence comes from an experiment Staub did in 1970: Children who voluntarily shared their candy turned out to have a lower need for approval than those who didn't share.

"If I'm feeling good about myself, I can respond to the needs of others," Staub explains. So helping needn't be motivated by a desire for approval.

• Do we help just to ease our own distress? Sometimes our motivation is undoubtedly like that of Hobbes. But the easiest way to stop feeling bad about someone else's suffering is "just to ignore it or leave," says Arizona State University psychologist Nancy Eisenberg. Instead we often stay and help, and "there's no reason to believe we do that just to make ourselves feel better."

When people are distressed over another person's pain they may help—for selfish reasons. But if they have the chance simply to turn away from the cause of their distress, they'll gladly do that instead. People who choose to help when they have the opportunity to pass by, like the biblical Good Samaritan, aren't motivated by their own discomfort. And these people, according to C. Daniel Batson, a psychologist at the University of Kansas, describe their feelings as compassionate and sympathetic rather than anxious and apprehensive.

Batson explored this behavior by having students listen to a radio news broadcast about a college senior whose parents had just been killed in a car accident. The students who responded most empathically to her problem also offered the most help, even though it would have been easy for them to say no and put the whole thing out of their minds.

• Do we help just to feel pleased with ourselves or to avoid guilt? The obvious way to test this, Batson argues, is to see how we feel after learning that "someone else" has come to a victim's aid. If we really cared only about patting ourselves on the back (or escaping twinges of guilt), we would insist on being the rescuer. But sometimes we are concerned only to make sure that the person who needs help gets it, regardless of who does the helping. That suggests a truly altruistic motivation. . . .

Batson, incidentally, used to assume that we help others primarily to benefit ourselves. But after a decade of studying empathic response to distress, he's changed his mind. "I feel like the bulk of the evidence points in the direction of the existence of altruism," he says.

Altruism in Children

• If we're naturally selfish, why does helping behavior start so early in life? At the age of 10 to 14 months, a baby will often look upset when someone else falls down or cries. Obviously made unhappy by another person's unhappiness, the child may seek solace in the mother's lap. In the second year, the child will begin comforting in a rudimentary way, such as by patting the head of someone who seems to be in pain. "The frequency (of this behavior) will vary, but most kids will do it sometimes," says Eisenberg.

By the time children are 3 or 4, prosocial behavior is common. One group of researchers videotaped 26 3- to 5-year-olds during 30 hours of free play and recorded about 1,200 acts of sharing, helping, comforting and cooperating. Children can be selfish and mean, too, of course, but there's no reason to think that these characteristics are more common or "natural" than their prosocial inclinations.

Psychologist Hoffman points to two studies showing that newborns cried much more intensely at the sound of another baby's cry than at other, equally loud noises. "That isn't what I'd call empathy," he concedes, "but it is evidence of a primitive precursor to it. There's a basic human tendency to be responsive to other persons' needs, not just your own."

Selfish Genes?

Hoffman rejects biological theories that claim altruism amounts to nothing more than "selfish genes" trying to preserve themselves by prompting the individual to help relatives who share those genes. But he does believe "there may be a biological basis for a disposition to altruism. Natural selection demanded that humans evolve as creatures disposed toward

The Necessity of Connection

In our highly individualistic culture, we tend to uphold a romantic vision of the altruistic hero, a lone, isolated individual who stands against the tide for what is right, indifferent to what others think. And yet few if any of those we studied represented this stereotype. Rather, they cared what others thought and felt, and were characterized by a particular capacity for connection, an ability to draw others around them into communities of comfort and challenge.

Anne Sanchez, working for years to involve disaffected citizens in the political process, said, "You don't make it on your own, and in my experience, the people who tried were the people who lost their commitments." Without the knowledge that we are intrinsically connected with one another, our effectiveness is sharply limited, and we are ill-equipped for the long haul in the face of the inevitable difficulties that arise when we do have to stand up for what is right.

Larry Parks Daloz,
Yes! Magazine, *Fall 1999.*

helping, rescuing, protecting others in danger" as well as toward looking out for their own needs.

According to Hoffman, the inborn mechanism that forms the basis for altruism is empathy, which he defines as feeling something more appropriate to someone else's situation than to your own. The way he sees it, empathy becomes increasingly more sophisticated as we grow. First, infants are unable to draw sharp boundaries between themselves and others and sometimes react to another's distress as if they, themselves, had been hurt.

By about 18 months, children can distinguish between "me" and "not-me" but will still assume that others' feelings will be similar to their own. That's why if Jason sees his mother cry out in pain, he may fetch his bottle to make her feel better. By age 2 or 3, it is possible to understand that others react differently and also to empathize with more complex emotions.

Finally, older children can feel for another person's life condition, understanding that his or her distress may be chronic or recognizing that the distress may result from being part of a class of people who are oppressed.

Other psychologists, meanwhile, believe that you are more likely to help others not only if you feel their pain but also if you understand the way the world looks to them. This is called "role-taking" or "perspective-taking." "When people put themselves in the shoes of others, they may become more inclined to render them aid," according to Canadian researchers Dennis Krebs and Cristine Russell.

When they asked an 8-year-old boy named Adam whether that seemed right to him, he replied as follows: "Oh yes, what you do is, you forget everything else that's in your head, and then you make your mind into their mind. Then you know how they're feeling, so you know how to help them."

Some people seem more inclined than others to take Adam's advice—and, in general, to be prosocially oriented. Staub has found that such people have three defining characteristics: They have a positive view of people in general, they are concerned about others' welfare and they take personal responsibility for how other people are doing.

All these, but particularly the first, are affected by the kind of culture one lives in. "It's difficult to lead a competitive, individualistic life"—as we're raised to do in American society—"without devaluing others to some extent," says Staub. So raising children to triumph over others in school and at play is a good way to snuff out their inclination to help.

It appears, then, that caring about others is as much a part of human nature as caring about ourselves. Which impulse gets emphasized is a matter of training, according to the experts. "We fundamentally have the potential to develop into caring, altruistic people or violent, aggressive people," says Staub. "No one will be altruistic if their experiences teach them to be concerned only about themselves. But human connection is intrinsically satisfying if we allow it to be."

"First take decent care of yourself, and then you can turn to those who deserve your help."

Self-Interest Promotes Moral Behavior

Tibor R. Machan

Tibor R. Machan teaches at the Argyros School of Business and Economics at Chapman University in Orange, California. He is also the author of Initiative: Human Agency and Society. *In the following viewpoint, Machan argues that authentic morality is rooted in self-interest rather than altruism. Only when we have tended to our own needs first can we be of genuine benefit to others, he maintains. Those who act altruistically may mean well, but unless their actions yield good results, their intentions are worthless. But when we help ourselves first, we are generally more successful at helping others, Machan concludes.*

As you read, consider the following questions:

1. What analogy does Tibor R. Machan use to illustrate the morality of self-interest?

2. In the author's opinion, why does Mother Teresa's moral system deserve criticism?

3. Why is altruism so widely praised, according to Machan?

Now, I am the last guy on earth to take my clues about life from government regulators. Yet, there are exceptions even to this rule: I ran across one candidate on a recent flight from Orange County to San Jose, California.

If you've ever flown, you probably remember the flight attendants' emergency instructions, delivered before each take-off: "If we lose air pressure, the oxygen mask will drop from above, and, if you are sitting next to a child, first apply the mask to yourself and then help the kid," or something to that effect. This is one of the few examples in popular culture where it is recognized that, in order to be an effective beneficiary to other people who need one's assistance, one must first be good to oneself—to have rendered oneself fit and able to help. In other words, even the most altruistic sentiments can only bear fruit after certain egoistic needs have been satisfied.

Help Yourself First

No doubt the matter is a bit more complicated. Those who believe that our lives ought first and foremost be devoted to helping the needy believe that what counts most is what we intend to result from our conduct. This is often expressed as the platitude "It's the thought that counts." But, of course, no help that is merely intended achieves very much. What matters is whether the help actually yields results. As it turns out, help toward others that isn't preceded by help toward oneself cannot very often succeed. Inept, unskilled, merely well-meaning folks tend to be of little use to themselves or others.

While many preachers of morality endorse altruism, even they sometimes realize that, unless you love and thus care for yourself first, you cannot love anyone else very effectively. For example, take psychology: The therapies and self-help programs to which millions flock usually make no bones about

Humans Are Fundamentally Self-Interested

Human beings appear to be intrinsically concerned first with their own welfare.

Hans Selye has argued that the desire to maintain oneself and stay happy is the most ancient—and one of the most important—impulses that motivates living beings. All living beings protect their own interests first of all. Selye points out that this begins with our basic biological make-up, in that the various cells in our bodies only cooperate with each other to ensure their own survival. . . .

It appears that like self-interest, social interest is also inherent within human beings—both have biological roots. Collaboration between body cells promotes the survival of each individual cell and enables the total organism to function.

In effect, individual interests are best served by mutual cooperation. Accordingly, self-interest without social interest is misguided. So is social interest without self-interest. Always putting others first leads to resentment or a martyr attitude. People who believe they are acting purely in the interests of others are dangerous. By denying (to themselves) that their own self-interest is involved, such people may justify all types of manipulative and controlling behavior toward others.

You are both self-interested and socially interested. This dual tendency is built in to your very being and begins with your basic biology. By accepting this about yourself, you will be able to do a better job of acting in your own interests—in an enlightened manner.

"Enlightened Self," Smart Recovery Online, *2004.*

advocating out-and-out selfishness—of a decent variety, to be sure, not some crass, fictional, brutal selfishness of the sort presented in bad movies like *Erin Brockovich* or *Wall Street.* Instead, most therapies and self-help regimens encourage people to be good to themselves in intelligent, nondestructive ways. No one is met by his or her shrink with the words, "Now let me help you over the next several months to get you to practice effective self-sacrifice!" Any such practitioners would lose their lucrative jobs in a jiffy if they did that, and rightly so.

Mother Teresa Versus Bill Gates

But, in the moral system most commonly preached, the story goes otherwise. Mother Teresa was the saint she was, not because she did well for herself—although she did keep saying that she drew great satisfaction from her work, as do most folks who have made it their vocation to help others—but because she meant well for others. It may be, as some have suggested, that Bill Gates is actually doing much more for humanity than Mother Teresa ever did, by creating jobs and tools by which the lives of millions have improved measurably. But because he presumably did this, at least initially, so as to enrich himself, it doesn't count for much in the calculus of popular moral ideals. The fact that Mother Teresa merely helped folks to get by from one day to the next and never tried to set them on some long-term successful course of living doesn't matter, so long as she meant well!

Such a moral system, which actually results in dependence and personal ineptitude unless confined to mere emergency situations, bears serious scrutiny and, yes, criticism. That federally mandated announcement made on every passenger plane gives us a clue as to how a genuine morality must operate: First take decent care of yourself, and then you can turn to those who deserve your help. Practiced conscientiously by everyone, this makes much better sense than the far more popular altruism to which most people give lip service.

Results Matter Most

One thing remains to ponder: If altruism is impractical and confusing, why is it so widely preached? The answer may be that, when moral matters are considered publicly, we tend to focus on what other people can do for us. Nice folks do good service; we thank them when they help us out, whereas if they do well for themselves, we tend not to notice. It matters little to me that you are good to yourself but rather how nice you are to me. So when public debate turns to moral matters, the focus drifts toward generosity, benevolence, charity—the virtues of intention—and away from prudence, courage, and moderation, the virtues that aid one toward self-improvement. And so the part of morality that guides us in our relationships to other people tends to get top billing and people mistake the part for the whole.

However, on airplanes—and anywhere else where it is results, not intentions, that matter most—then the wiser course is clear: First genuinely love yourself; then only can you be an effective lover of others!

For Further Discussion

Chapter 1

1. In his viewpoint M. Scott Peck discusses transference, which he defines as the inappropriate application of a childhood view of the world to the adult environment. He also speculates on the role transference may play in community and international relationships—such as how Americans' experiences during the 1930s and 1940s may have influenced the way American leaders waged war in Vietnam. Do you see possible examples of transference in national and international affairs today? What are they? Do you think that today's world leaders may be influenced by their childhood ways of perceiving and responding to the world? Why or why not? Cite specific passages from the text in your response.

2. Imagine that Plato visited you and addressed his allegory of the cave to you directly, with the cave being a description of your life and your world. What insights would his allegory give you? In your life situation, what might the terms "shadows," "light," "ascent," and "sight" symbolize? Cite specific passages from the text in your response.

3. M. Scott Peck uses the image of the map, Plato uses the metaphor of the cave, and Sam Keen uses the idea of myth to help people better understand their lives and the nature of truth. Which metaphor do you believe provides the best guidance for constructing a life philosophy? Explain. Cite specific passages from the text(s) in your response.

4. Charles Larmore challenges the common philosophical notion that "the life lived well is the life lived in accord

with a rational plan." In your opinion, does Larmore's viewpoint negate or enhance the concept of constructing a life philosophy? Use citations from the chapter as you compose your answer.

Chapter 2

1. Richard Robinson rejects the existence of God. For this reason he concludes that we must create our own purpose in life and "behave brotherly to each other" in light of humanity's insecurity and inevitable extinction. George E. Saint-Laurent maintains that religious believers often commune with the sacred by dying to self, giving alms, and serving the needy. In your opinion, does Robinson's atheistic humanism provide a more solid foundation than religion for promoting human welfare? Why or why not? Cite specific passages from the text(s) in your response.

2. Wayne Anderson argues that science is preferable to religion in pursuing the meaning of life. Sharon Begley maintains that both science and religion can illuminate the mysteries of the cosmos. What supporting arguments do the authors use to back up their conclusions? On what points do they agree? On what points do they disagree? In the end, whose argument do you find more compelling? Use evidence from the text as you explain your answer.

Chapter 3

1. Philip Yancey maintains that without the guidance of religion, people have no way of distinguishing between right and wrong. Do you agree with his argument that religion is the only reliable guide to determining what is

right and wrong? What alternative view does Frank R. Zindler propose? Cite specific passages from the text(s) in your response.

2. Paul Kurtz argues that secular humanism provides a "method for the explanation and discovery of rational moral principles." How do you think John Gray would respond to Kurtz's assertion? Which author's argument do you think is more convincing? Cite passages from the viewpoints to support your conclusions.

3. After reading the viewpoints by Alfie Kohn and Tibor R. Machan, what are your thoughts about the psychological motivations for helping others? Do you agree with Kohn that the desire to benefit others is largely rooted in altruism, or do you accept Machan's belief that truly moral actions begin with self-interest? Or do you think that both altruism and self-interest prompt moral behavior? Give specific examples to support your claim.

Periodical Bibliography

The following articles have been selected to supplement the diverse views presented in this chapter.

Cohen, S. Mark. Lecture Notes: The Allegory of the Cave. 16 June 2009. http://faculty.washington.edu/smcohen/320/cave.htm.

Garrett, Alexander. "Buying Time to Do the Things That Really Matter." *Management Today*. (July 2000): 75.

Gini, Al. "Work, Identity and Self: How We Are Formed by the Work We Do." *Journal of Business Ethics* 17.7 (May 1998): 707–14.

Levy, Neil. "Downshifting and Meaning in Life." *Ratio* 18 (June 2, 2005): 176–89.

"The Meaningful Life," *Positive Psychology*. Harvard Health Publications Group (March 2009): 28.

Miller, Laura. "'The Matrix and Philosophy' by William Irwin, ed." Book Review. December 4, 2002. http://dir.salon.com/story/books/review/2002/12/04/matrix/index.html.

Morris, Tom. "Living in Plato's Cave." March 24, 2009. Huffingtonpost.com.

Nielan, Cate. "William Blank: The Meaning of Life." December 2003. *Intercom: The Magazine of the Society for Technical Communication*, December 2003.

Pihlström, Sami. "A Meaningful Life in a Meaningless Cosmos?: Two Rival Approaches." *Cosmos and History* 3.1 (January 2007): 4–17.

Rohn, Jim. "Your Philosophy, the Cornerstone of Total and Lasting Success; Your Personal Philosophy Is the Greatest Determining Factor in How Your Life Works Out." *Success*, (April–May 2009): 72–75.

Taylor, Ken. "Intergenerational Obligations and the Rope of Lives." Philosophy Talk, The Blog. June 8, 2005. http://theblog.philosophytalk.org/.

OPPOSING
VIEWPOINTS®
SERIES

Should Limits Be Placed on Freedom of Expression?

Chapter Preface

In 1981 a fourteen-year-old boy was found by his mother and his best friend hanging by a belt in his closet. At his feet lay a copy of *Hustler* magazine open to an article titled "Orgasm of Death," which described autoerotic asphyxiation. A form of masturbation, autoerotic asphyxiation involves restricting air supply at the moment of orgasm to allegedly experience more intense pleasure. The boy's mother and his friend sued the magazine in *Herceg v. Hustler Magazine, Inc.* for causing fatal injury to a child, thus violating Texas law. Although federal jurors decided for the plaintiff, the case was overturned in 1987 by the Fifth U.S. Circuit Court of Appeals, which argued that the article fell within the magazine's right to freedom of speech. This case represents the enormous controversy over whether pornography and other forms of speech often considered harmful deserve constitutional protection.

According to the Community Defense Council (CDC), an anti-pornography organization, three categories of speech are not protected by the First Amendment: libel, fighting words (speech intended to inflict injury or disturb the peace), and obscenity. In 1973, in *Miller v. California*, the Supreme Court outlined a three-part test that almost every state uses to identify obscenity. For an expression to be obscene, the Court decided that the average person of the affected community must find that the expression appeals directly to prurient interests, the expression must be patently offensive, and the expression must lack redeeming value. Anti-pornography crusaders contend that pornographic material, such as the *Hustler* article, passes the *Miller* test for obscenity, and thus does not deserve constitutional protection under the First Amendment.

In the dissenting opinion in *Herceg*, Justice Edith H. Jones argued that *Hustler* magazine should have been held responsible for the boy's death. She criticized the fact that First

Amendment jurisprudence serves to protect individuals from "defamation, obscenity, and the threat of mob violence," but, in this case, it failed to protect individuals from bodily harm and death caused by speech. Jones and others contend that because pornography does not contribute to any productive exchange of ideas, it should not be afforded full First Amendment protection. As stated by the CDC, "Incredibly, the majority [in *Herceg*] decided that a pornographic magazine's article which explains in great detail how to masturbate while cutting off oxygen to the brain, and which led to the death of a teenager, was entitled to just as much protection under the First Amendment as pure political speech."

Others argue that pornography must be accorded full First Amendment protection to ensure that all forms of expression remain free. Nadine Strossen, president of the American Civil Liberties Union (ACLU), contends that any restriction on expression jeopardizes existing free speech protections. For example, she argues, if pornography is censored, "the government could outlaw flag burning and the teaching of Marxist doctrine because they might lead to the erosion of patriotism and our capitalist system . . . [and] advertising for alcohol, tobacco, and innumerable other products could be prohibited because it might cause adverse health effects." Thus, according to Strossen, censoring pornography because of its potential for harm could lead to the censoring of all forms of expression that carry risks.

The debate over whether pornography should receive First Amendment protection reflects the controversial nature of expression in a free society. According to free expression advocates, limiting speech to popular ideas risks silencing controversial, but possibly beneficial, voices. Justice Alvin Rubin, writing the majority opinion in *Herceg*, stated, "The constitutional protection accorded to the freedom of speech and of the press is not based on the naïve belief that speech can do no harm, but on the confidence that the benefits society reaps from the free flow and exchange of ideas outweigh the costs society endures by receiving reprehensible or dangerous ideas."

The debate over pornography and free speech has been a long-standing one. Indeed, issues regarding free expression evoke powerful emotions in a nation that calls itself "the land of the free." Authors in the following chapter debate how much freedom of expression should be limited to protect society without destroying the freedom that Americans hold so dear.

> "When freedom of expression is stretched to protect . . . advertising, gossip, racial slurs, obscenity, and pornography with a blind eye and an even hand, the whole concept loses its credibility."

Limits Should Be Placed on Freedom of Expression

Francis Canavan

According to Canavan in the following viewpoint, the First Amendment does not guarantee absolute freedom of expression. He maintains that the First Amendment only applies to freedom of speech and freedom of the press, not to all expression. Modern liberals, he argues, contend that free expression is valuable in itself, regardless of what is expressed. In Canavan's opinion, however, free expression is only valuable when it contributes to the good of society. Thus, free speech and free press are the means to a social good, not a good in themselves, and can be restricted to serve that good, Canavan contends. Canavan is the author of several books on political theory, including The Ethical Dimension of Political Life *and* Freedom of Expression: Purpose as Limit.

Francis Canavan, "Speech That Matters," *Society*, vol. 36, September 1999, p. 11. Copyright © 1999 by Transaction Publishers.

As you read, consider the following questions:

1. Whose power to censure does the First Amendment apply to, according to Francis Canavan?

2. In the author's opinion, why did historic figures, such as John Milton and John Stuart Mill, advocate freedom of speech and the press?

3. As stated by Canavan, what is society's greatest need today?

Everyone knows that the First Amendment to the Constitution of the United States guarantees the freedom of speech and press. Many people, however, intellectuals not the least among them, do not know what the First Amendment actually says. They are convinced nonetheless that it means something that it does not in fact say and cannot mean. As Will Rogers used to say, the trouble with this country is that too many people know too many things that just ain't so.

Limitations on Government

For example, it is widely and unthinkingly believed that the First Amendment prohibits all constraint on speech or publication imposed by anyone. In fact, however, the Amendment speaks only of the U.S. Congress: "*Congress* (emphasis added) shall make no law . . . abridging the freedom of speech, or of the press." Through its interpretation of the Fourteenth Amendment, the U.S. Supreme Court has extended this limitation of Congress's power to all levels of government in the United States—but only to governments. The First Amendment limits what governments may do, not what private institutions or individuals may do in regard to speech or publication. As the Court remarked in *Hudgens v. NLRB [National Labor Relations Board]* . . . in 1976,

It is a commonplace that the constitutional guarantee of free speech is a guarantee only against abridgment by government, federal, or state.

Well-informed people are aware that the Amendment applies only to governments, but some of them argue that governments, at least, are barred from imposing any limitation on anything that can be called "expression." These First Amendment absolutists, as we may call them, collapse "the freedom of speech, or of the press" into "freedom of expression." They then assume that anything that comes out of a human mouth, a printing press, or a motion picture projector, or is done in a theatrical performance, is "expression." As such, they allege, it is immune from interference by government. . . .

Expression Versus Conduct

Freedom of speech and press is too complex a notion to be condensed into absolute freedom of expression. Yet absolutists continually try to turn the First Amendment into a guarantee of freedom of expression without limit or qualification. In their view, it does not matter what is expressed, or how it is expressed, so long as it is "expressed" and not "done." According to them, no legislature and no court may consider the substantive content of an utterance or publication because to do so would engage government in "censorship." The content of expression is thus absorbed into its form: From a constitutional point of view, the content is irrelevant and all that matters is that it has the form of expression rather than the form of conduct.

But to take this position is to detach expression from any ends which it may be supposed to serve and to make it an end in itself. We give constitutional protection to speech and publication, the argument runs, not for any good we hope to achieve through them, but simply for the sake of expression, which is considered as a good in and of itself. The right to expression is absolute because expression is the end and is not a means to any higher end which might limit it.

This point is crucial because ends both justify and limit means. That the end justifies the means is a classically immoral principle if it is understood to mean that a good end justifies any means, however evil in itself. But there is a perfectly legitimate sense in which only an end can justify a means. If you ask someone why he is using a certain instrument or following a certain course of action, he explains and justifies what he is doing by telling you what he is trying to accomplish, why it is a good thing to accomplish, and how this instrument or policy is designed to achieve that end. In this sense the end justifies the means and nothing but the end can justify it insofar as it is a means.

The relationship of end and means bears directly on the question why we Americans, or any other sane and civilized people, should want a national policy of freedom of speech and press. Absolutists badly assert that we treasure expression as an end in itself and tell us that is The American Way. We guarantee everyone's right to express whatever he feels like expressing, without regard to the content, manner, or medium of expression, and without regard to the public health, safety, welfare, or morals, simply and solely because it is expression and expression deserves protection for its own sake. Expression is the end and the end is pursued without limit.

Now it may be well that no one ever goes quite that far in advocating absolute freedom of expression, although it must be admitted that the rhetoric which some advocates use goes far in that direction. Still, if pressed, most absolutists will qualify their demand to some extent. But the moment qualifications are admitted, we have to cease to regard expression as an absolute end and have begun to look on it in relation to ends and consequences beyond itself.

The Value of Expression

There are evils which we are not prepared to tolerate merely because preventing them would involve some limitation of expression. There are social goods to which certain forms of expression seem to have no relation at all and it is not clear why those forms of expression deserve protection. At this point we must ask ourselves what value we attach to expression as such. Granted, we do place some value on the right to speak freely; the question is how much? Do we see this right as a primary end, to which all else is subordinate, or do we consider freedom of expression as valuable principally for the service it renders to ends beyond itself?

If we answer yes to the latter question, that is, if we view freedom of speech and press principally as a means to higher and further ends, then we shall find it difficult to justify an unlimited freedom of expression. For ends not only justify but limit means. No one who rationally pursues an end chooses and keeps on using means which turn out not to achieve it, or to be irrelevant to it, or positively to impede its accomplishment. The end governs the choice and use of means and limits the means to those which really promote the end.

So, at least, have the major historical advocates of freedom of speech and press always understood it. John Milton, Benedict de Spinoza, John Stuart Mill, and such lesser but significant luminaries as Tunis Wortman, Walter Bagehot, Harold Laski, Zechariah Chafee Jr., and Alexander Meiklejohn, have all argued for a broad freedom of speech and press. But the argument was that freedom to speak and publish liberated human reason to pursue truth, that the truth would reveal to men what was good for them, and that the good would make them happy. The true and the good were the end, reason was the means for achieving it, and freedom of speech and press was the necessary condition for reason to do its work.

Pursuing Truth

These men were all, in varying degrees, optimistic rationalists. Their faith in the power of reason may have been exaggerated, but it was the rock on which they built their case for freedom of expression. They did not build it on the value of expression simply as expression, and certainly not on a skeptical doubt about the ability of the human mind to know truth.

They did not think that the truth was immediately and without effort known to all. On the contrary, truth had to be laboriously pursued and the pursuit was more likely to be successful if it engaged many minds in controversy and debate. Milton stated this conviction in famous and oft-quoted lines in his *Areopagitica*:

> Though all the winds of doctrine were let loose to play upon the earth, so Truth be in the field, we do injuriously by licensing and prohibiting to misdoubt her strength. Let her and Falsehood grapple: who ever knew Truth put to the worse, in a free and open encounter.

Truth is great and will prevail, but not at once. The "golden rule," Milton assures us, is "to be still searching for what we know not, by what we know, still closing up truth to truth as we find it."

In *Tractatus Politicus* Benedict de Spinoza advocated in similar terms for men's freedom to speak their minds on questions of public importance:

> Human wits are too blunt to get to the heart of all problems immediately; but they are sharpened by the give and take of discussion and debate, and by exploring every possible course men eventually discover the measures which all approve and which no one would have thought of before discussion.

Lacking Absolute Certainty

John Stuart Mill is often thought of as basing his pleas for unrestrained freedom of discussion on skepticism because the premise of his argument was that we can never have "absolute certainty" and therefore never can be sure but that the opinion we suppress may be true. In fact, however, the conclusion he reached was not that truth was unknowable. Rather, it was that we would achieve a growing consensus on true opinions if we renounced all pretensions to infallibility and left the public forum open to all views, however immoral we might consider them to be (see *On Liberty*). Truth, though never known infallibly, was still great and would prevail. In *On Liberty* Mill writes:

> As mankind improves, the number of doctrines which are no longer disputed or doubted will be constantly on the increase; and the well-being of mankind may almost be measured by the number and gravity of the truths which have reached the point of being uncontested. . . .

In his book *Political Freedom: The Constitutional Powers of the People*, Meiklejohn held that the First Amendment provides an absolute guarantee of freedom only to political speech, i.e., to "speech which bears, directly or indirectly, upon issues with which voters have to deal—only, therefore, to the consideration of matters of public interest." In this forum he said, "Free men need truth as they need nothing else. In the last resort it is only the search for and dissemination of truth that can keep our country safe." Other kinds of speech can be and often have been limited by law; after mentioning some of them, he said, "this listing of legitimate legislative abridgments of speech could be continued indefinitely. Their number is legion." He acknowledged, "a private need to speak" which was entitled to "impartial consideration," but it was "liable to such abridgments as the general welfare may require."

Meiklejohn put his finger on the root defect of contemporary liberal thought (and, to some extent, of our constitutional jurisprudence besides) on the freedom of speech and press. It is the refusal to make distinctions among kinds and levels of speech and publication. Liberalism treats all manners of expressing oneself, from the most obscene to the most civilized, as identical, and it pretends that all media of expression—the spoken word, the printed word, the motion picture, and the live performance on stage—should be exactly the same in the eyes of the law.

Rejecting Reason

Even more radically, liberals today are constantly tempted to deny that there is any principle which reason can discern in the light of which we can make distinctions among the degrees of protection to which several kinds, manners and media of expression are entitled. The classical liberal argument for the freedom of speech and the press was founded on faith in reason. Today's liberal argument rejects the appeal to reason for fear lest, if it were admitted that reason can bring us to truth, then truth may become the ground for imposing restrictions on freedom. Better, it is thought, to defend an absolute and unqualified freedom of expression (or, if qualified, only by the need to stop short of direct incitement to crime) on the ground that truth is unattainable, that reason is no more than an instrument for finding the means to the satisfaction of desire, and that all expressions, no matter what they express or how they express it, are equal in the only essential respect, that of being expressions rather than actions.

In this radically subjective and skeptical view there is no distinction between speech that matters and speech that does not. No distinction is possible because there are no publicly acknowledged ends which the constitutionally guaranteed freedom of expression is supposed to serve. Since there are no ends to be achieved, there can be no limits on expression as a means to those ends.

But if this is so, there is also no answer to the question why we as a people should guarantee freedom of speech and press. If it serves no ends, why should we judge it so important that we write protection for it into our Constitution? Any answer would have to be stated in terms of the ends we hope to achieve, and contemporary liberals are left with no answer but this: We guarantee freedom of expression for its own sake. Expression is the end; reason, truth, and the public good have nothing to do with it.

But this is no answer, if one wishes to convince a whole people with it. Writers, artists, academicians, and intellectuals generally may value, or may think they value, freedom of expression above all other human goods. For their own reasons, so may journalists, gossip-mongers, and pornographers. Most people, however, do not rank an unqualified freedom of expression so highly as to sacrifice anything they consider truly important to it. When freedom of expression is stretched to protect not only religious preaching, political debate, scientific publication, and art, but also advertising, gossip, racial slurs, obscenity, and pornography with a blind eye and an even hand, the whole concept loses its credibility. Detached from the high and noble ends originally proposed for it, freedom of speech and press cannot be taken seriously.

The Public Good

Two positions remain to which First Amendment absolutists may fall back to answer to this criticism. One is that all expressions contribute in some way to the pursuit of truth and the public good. Bad ideas can be recognized as bad, but they still perform a useful function by calling forth good ideas in reply, and the public emerges wiser and better informed from the debate. That was the classical liberal argument. The contemporary liberal gloss on it, however, is that anything that can be uttered, printed, or presented on stage or screen is an idea and therefore a contribution to the rational goals of freedom. In light of what we can see, hear, and read today, this contention is simply unbelievable, and is in fact a return to the claim that expression is an end in itself.

Censure and Censorship

The fact that a wide variety of ideas can be expressed in our society does not mean they are all equally valid. Too many people believe that supporting freedom of expression means accepting, without judgment, all forms and content of free expression. As author Garry Wills has pointed out, "The whole idea of free speech is not to make certain ideas exempt from criticism but to expose them to it." There is a difference between censure and censorship. We have every right, perhaps even the obligation, to censure ideas we do not approve of. While someone may have the right to express a disturbing idea, he does not have the right to hide behind the First Amendment to avoid the heat of opposition. Limits in any society are the result of continuing dialog concerning what is and is not acceptable.

William H. Hogeboom,
Billboard, *March 27, 1993.*

The other fallback position (which was John Stuart Mill's ultimate line of defense) is that the harm done by allowing any restriction on expression always outweighs the good accomplished by it. Defenders of this position will admit that much of what is published in the several media today is trash not worth protecting, or is a corrupting influence that should be suppressed if it were possible to do so without suppressing valuable publications in the process. Unfortunately, however, they say, it is not possible: A government that can punish obscenity will end by banning Shakespeare and the Bible because they contain naughty words.

But this argument loses its persuasive power after a certain point. It is true that we must tolerate much that is foolish, offensive, and noxious lest in the effort to get rid of it, we should deprive ourselves of expressions which contribute to the purposes for which we have established freedom of speech and press. It does not follow that society must tolerate all expressions, however mindless or pernicious they may be, merely because First Amendment absolutists assure us that society is incapable of making rational distinctions among expressions.

There is, in fact, no reason to believe that such is the case. We know that arts and letters do not flourish under totalitarian tyrannies, but history provides no evidence to show that they flourish best under regimes of unlimited freedom of expression. The history of our own country, in particular during the permissive atmosphere of the past two decades, offers no ground for believing that the level of thought, discussion, literature, art, and even entertainment rises as the cultural and legal restraints on publication go down. The claim that freedom to think, speak, write, and present depends on the absence of all restraints is mere dogmatism.

Endangering Freedom

As Walter Lippmann explained more than thirty years ago in his book *Essays in the Public Philosophy*, this dogmatism endangers the very freedom it purports to defend:

> Divorced from its original purpose and justification, as a process of criticism, freedom to think and speak are not self-evident necessities. It is only from the hope and the intention of discovering truth that freedom acquires such high public significance.... The right to utter words, whether or not they have meaning, and regardless of their truth, could not be a vital interest of a great state but for the presumption that they are the chaff which goes with the utterance of true and significant words.

Our greatest need today is not to shove back ever farther the boundaries of free speech, but to remember why speech matters at all. We shall then recognize that not everything that can be called speech or expression really does matter.

> *"Without [freedom of expression], other fundamental rights, like the right to vote, would wither and die."*

Limits Should Not Be Placed on Freedom of Expression

American Civil Liberties Union

In the following viewpoint, the American Civil Liberties Union (ACLU) argues that protecting free expression is essential to maintaining a free society. According to the ACLU, the First Amendment protects "pure speech"—spoken and printed materials—and "symbolic speech"—nonverbal expression that includes flag burning and works of art. The ACLU maintains that even unpopular forms of expression, such as hate speech, should be protected to ensure the free flow of ideas. The ACLU is a nonprofit agency that protects civil rights and civil liberties.

As you read, consider the following questions:

1. As noted by the author, why was Sidney Street jailed in 1969?

2. What is the "Brandenburg standard," according to the author?

American Civil Liberties Union, "Freedom of Expression," ACLU Briefing Paper, 1997. Copyright © 1997 ACLU, 125 Broad Street, 18th Floor New York, NY 10004. Reproduced by permission.

3. As stated by the ACLU, what kind of political protest is not protected by the First Amendment?

Freedom of speech, of the press, of association, of assembly and petition—this set of guarantees, protected by the First Amendment, comprises what we refer to as freedom of expression. The Supreme Court has written that this freedom is "the matrix, the indispensable condition of nearly every other form of freedom." Without it, other fundamental rights, like the right to vote, would wither and die.

But in spite of its "preferred position" in our constitutional hierarchy, the nation's commitment to freedom of expression has been tested over and over again. Especially during times of national stress, like war abroad or social upheaval at home, people exercising their First Amendment rights have been censored, fined, even jailed. Those with unpopular political ideas have always borne the brunt of government repression. It was during WWI—hardly ancient history—that a person could be jailed just for giving out anti-war leaflets. Out of those early cases, modern First Amendment law evolved. Many struggles and many cases later, ours is the most speech-protective country in the world.

The path to freedom was long and arduous. It took nearly 200 years to establish firm constitutional limits on the government's power to punish "seditious" and "subversive" speech. Many people suffered along the way, such as labor leader Eugene V. Debs, who was sentenced to 10 years in prison under the Espionage Act just for telling a rally of peaceful workers to realize they were "fit for something better than slavery and cannon fodder." Or Sidney Street, jailed in 1969 for burning an American flag on a Harlem street corner to protest the shooting of civil rights figure James Meredith.

Free speech rights still need constant, vigilant protection. New questions arise and old ones return. Should flag burning be a crime? What about government or private censorship of works of art that touch on sensitive issues like religion or sexuality? Should the Internet be subject to any form of government control? What about punishing college students who espouse racist or sexist opinions? In answering these questions, the history and the core values of the First Amendment should be our guide.

The Supreme Court and the First Amendment

During our nation's early era, the courts were almost universally hostile to political minorities' First Amendment rights; free speech issues did not even reach the Supreme Court until 1919 when, in *Schenck v. United States*, the Court unanimously upheld the conviction of a Socialist Party member for mailing leaflets to draft-age men. A turning point occurred a few months later in *Abrams v. United States*. Although the defendant's conviction under the Espionage Act for distributing anti-war leaflets was upheld, two dissenting opinions formed the cornerstone of our modern First Amendment law. Justices Oliver Wendell Holmes and Louis D. Brandeis argued speech could *only* be punished *if* it presented "a clear and present danger" of imminent harm. Mere political advocacy, they said, was protected by the First Amendment. Eventually, these justices were able to convince a majority of the Court to adopt the "clear and present danger test."

From then on, the right to freedom of expression grew more secure—until the 1950s and McCarthyism.[1] The Supreme Court fell prey to the witch-hunt mentality of that period, seriously weakening the "clear and present danger" test by holding that speakers could be punished if they advocated overthrowing the government—even if the danger of such an occurrence were both slight and remote. As a result, many political activists were prosecuted and jailed simply for advocat-

1. In the 1950s Senator Joseph McCarthy accused large numbers of U.S. officials of being Communists. His charges were never proven, and he was censured by the Senate in 1954.

ing Communist revolution. Loyalty oath requirements for government employees were upheld; thousands of Americans lost their jobs on the basis of flimsy evidence supplied by secret witnesses.

Finally, in 1969, in *Brandenburg v. Ohio*, the Supreme Court struck down the conviction of a Ku Klux Klan member, and established a new standard: Speech can be suppressed only if it is intended, *and likely to produce*, "imminent lawless action." Otherwise, even speech that advocates violence is protected. The Brandenburg standard prevails today.

What Does "Protected Speech" Include?

First Amendment protection is not limited to "pure speech"— books, newspapers, leaflets, and rallies. It also protects "symbolic speech"—nonverbal expression whose purpose is to communicate ideas. In its 1969 decision in *Tinker v. Des Moines*, the Court recognized the right of public school students to wear black armbands in protest of the Vietnam War. In 1989 (*Texas v. Johnson*) and again in 1990 (*United States v. Eichman*), the Court struck down government bans on "flag desecration." Other examples of protected symbolic speech include works of art, T-shirt slogans, political buttons, music lyrics and theatrical performances.

Government can limit some protected speech by imposing "time, place and manner" restrictions. This is most commonly done by requiring permits for meetings, rallies and demonstrations. But a permit cannot be unreasonably withheld, nor can it be denied based on content of the speech. That would be what is called viewpoint discrimination—and *that* is unconstitutional.

When a protest crosses the line from speech to action, the government can intervene more aggressively. Political protesters have the right to picket, to distribute literature, to chant

Three Reasons Why Freedom of Expression Is Essential to a Free Society

- It's the foundation of self-fulfillment. The right to express one's thoughts and to communicate freely with others affirms the dignity and worth of each and every member of society, and allows each individual to realize his or her full human potential. Thus, freedom of expression is an end in itself—and as such, deserves society's greatest protection.

- It's vital to the attainment and advancement of knowledge, and the search for the truth. The eminent 19th-century writer and civil libertarian, John Stuart Mill, contended that enlightened judgment is possible only if one considers all facts and ideas, from whatever source, and tests one's own conclusions against opposing views. Therefore, all points of view—even those that are "bad" or socially harmful—should be represented in society's "marketplace of ideas."

- It's necessary to our system of self-government and gives the American people a "checking function" against government excess and corruption. If the American people are to be the masters of their fate and of their elected government, they must be well-informed and have access to all information, ideas and points of view. Mass ignorance is a breeding ground for oppression and tyranny.

American Civil Liberties Union,
"Freedom of Expression," 1997.

and to engage passersby in debate. But they do not have the right to block building entrances or to physically harass people.

Free Speech for Hatemongers?

The ACLU [American Civil Liberties Union] has often been at the center of controversy for defending the free speech rights of groups that spew hate, such as the Ku Klux Klan and the Nazis. But if only popular ideas were protected, we wouldn't need a First Amendment. History teaches that the first target of government repression is never the last. If we do not come to the defense of the free speech rights of the most unpopular among us, even if their views are antithetical to the very freedom the First Amendment stands for, then no one's liberty will be secure. In that sense, all First Amendment rights are "indivisible."

Censoring so-called hate speech also runs counter to the long-term interests of the most frequent victims of hate: racial, ethnic, religious and sexual minorities. We should not give the government the power to decide which opinions are hateful, for history has taught us that government is more apt to use this power to prosecute minorities than to protect them. As one federal judge has put it, tolerating hateful speech is "the best protection we have against any Nazi-type regime in this country."

At the same time, freedom of speech does not prevent punishing conduct that intimidates, harasses, or threatens another person, even if words are used. Threatening phone calls, for example, are not constitutionally protected.

Speech and National Security

The Supreme Court has recognized the government's interest in keeping some information secret, such as wartime troop deployments. But the Court has never actually upheld an injunction against speech on national security grounds. Two lessons can be learned from this historical fact. First, the amount of speech that can be curtailed in the interest of national security is very limited. And second, the government has historically overused the concept of "national security" to shield itself from criticism, and to discourage public discussion of controversial policies or decisions.

In 1971, the publication of "The Pentagon Papers" by *The New York Times* brought the conflicting claims of free speech and national security to a head. "The Pentagon Papers," a voluminous secret history and analysis of the country's involvement in Vietnam, was leaked to the press. When the *Times* ignored the government's demand that it cease publication, the stage was set for a Supreme Court decision. In the landmark *New York Times Co. v. United States* case, the Court ruled that the government could not, through "prior restraint," block publication of any material unless it could prove that it would "surely" result in "direct, immediate, and irreparable" harm to the nation. This the government failed to prove, and the public was given access to vital information about an issue of enormous importance.

The public's First Amendment "right to know" is essential to its ability to fully participate in democratic decision making. As the "Pentagon Papers" case demonstrates, the government's claims of "national security" must always be closely scrutinized to make sure they are valid.

Unprotected Expression

The Supreme Court has recognized several limited exceptions to First Amendment protection.

- In *Chaplinsky v. New Hampshire* (1942), the Court held that so-called "fighting words . . . which by their very utterance inflict injury or tend to incite an immediate breach of the peace," are not protected. This decision was based on the fact that fighting words are of "slight social value as a step to truth."

- In *New York Times Co. v. Sullivan* (1964), the Court held that defamatory falsehoods about public officials can be punished—*only* if the offended official can prove the falsehoods were published with "actual malice," i.e.: "knowledge that the statement was false or with reckless disregard of whether it was false or not." Other kinds of "libelous statements" are also punishable.

- Legally "obscene" material has historically been excluded from First Amendment protection. Unfortunately, the relatively narrow obscenity exception, described below, has been abused by government authorities and private pressure groups. Sexual expression in art and entertainment is, and has historically been, the most frequent target of censorship crusades, from James Joyce's classic *Ulysses* to the photographs of Robert Mapplethorpe.

In the 1973 *Miller v. California* decision, the Court established three conditions that must be present if a work is to be deemed "legally obscene." It must 1) appeal to the average person's prurient (shameful, morbid) interest in sex; 2) depict sexual conduct in a "patently offensive way" as defined by community standards; and 3) taken as a whole, lack serious literary, artistic, political or scientific value. Attempts to apply the "Miller test" have demonstrated the impossibility of formulating a precise definition of obscenity. Justice Potter Stewart once delivered a famous one-liner on the subject: "I know it when I see it." But the fact is, the obscenity exception to the First Amendment is highly subjective and practically invites government abuse.

The ACLU: Ongoing Champion of Free Expression

The American Civil Liberties Union (ACLU) has been involved in virtually all of the landmark First Amendment cases to reach the U.S. Supreme Court, and remains absolutely committed to the preservation of each and every individual's freedom of expression. During the 1980s, we defended the right of artists and entertainers to perform and produce works of art free of government and private censorship. During the 1990s, the organization fought to protect free speech in cyberspace when state and federal government attempted to impose content-based regulations on the Internet. In addition, the ACLU offers several books on the subject of freedom of expression.

"It may be worth considering some very limited restrictions on some hate expression."

Hate Speech Should Be Regulated

Laura Leets

According to Laura Leets in the following viewpoint, some limits should be placed on hate speech because it may contribute to the incidence of hate crimes. Although hate speech usually does not have immediate consequences, it may eventually combine with other influences to incite people to commit hate crimes, she argues. Moreover, she contends that many racist or other extremist groups are communicating their messages of hate to unprecedented numbers of people via the Internet. Public officials should consider enacting restrictions on hateful expressions, particularly those communicated over the Internet, to minimize the effects of racism and hatred in society, Leets maintains. Leets is an assistant professor in the communications department at Stanford University.

As you read, consider the following questions:

1. As explained by the author, what is the difference between "deterministic causality" and "probabilistic causality"?

2. What is moral exclusion, as defined by Susan Opotow?

3. Why would regulating hate speech on the Internet be difficult, according to Laura Leets?

There's been a groundswell in the past several years to increase diversity in journalism, both in news coverage and in newsroom staffing. The goal of several diversity initiatives is to increase the number of voices that regularly appear in our newspapers, magazines, broadcasts and Web sites.

It's important to seek different perspectives and ideas, and the goal of such initiatives is an admirable and productive one. There are some voices, however, that have demonstrably adverse effects. So while the journalism community, judicial system and American public generally support tolerance of diverse viewpoints, some perspectives and types of speech still warrant concern.

The Rising Incidence of Hate Crimes

One problematic voice is that of hate. Whether it is the dragging death of an African American behind a pick-up truck in Texas, a gay student's murder in Wyoming, a racially motivated shooting spree at a Los Angeles Jewish community center or a bloody rampage by two high school students enamored of Hitler's fascism, the rising incidence of hate crimes and the groups who appear to encourage them is attracting public interest.[1] In particular, the World Wide Web has pro-

1. In 1998 African American James Byrd was chained to a pick-up truck and dragged to death. Gay college student Matthew Shepard was beaten and then tied to a post and left to die in Wyoming in 1998. In 1999 Buford O'Neal Furrow entered a Jewish Community Center in Los Angeles and opened fire, wounding five people, including three young children. At Columbine High School in Colorado in 1999, students Eric Harris and Dylan Klebold went on a shooting rampage, killing fifteen and wounding twenty-three others.

vided marginalized extremist groups a more notable and accessible public platform. The Internet has put the problem of incendiary hate into sharp relief.

In several research studies where I have focused on short-term message effects of hate speech, it is difficult to demonstrate with certainty the linkage between hate expression and violence or harm (deterministic causality). In a recent study, I asked 266 participants (both university and non-university students recruited online) to read and evaluate one of 11 white supremacist Web pages that I had randomly sampled from the Internet. Similar to previous studies, the data showed that the content of the hate Web pages was perceived to be in keeping with the Court bounds for First Amendment protection. Yet the participants acknowledged an indirect effect that, on the other hand, may suggest hate speech effects are more slow-acting—and thus imperceptible in the short term (probabilistic causality).

Specifically, participants in the cyberhate study rated the indirect threats from the World Church of the Creator (WCOTC) [a white supremacist organization] Web page as very high (Mean=6, on a seven-point scale where seven represented the highest score). Is it coincidental that a former WCOTC member . . . shot 11 Asian Americans, African Americans and Jews, killing two, before committing suicide? Or that two brothers associated with WCOTC were charged with murdering a gay couple and fire-bombing three Sacramento synagogues? While WCOTC leader Matthew Hale does not endorse this lawlessness, neither does he condemn it. Part of their ideology is that all nonwhites are "mud people," people without souls, like animals eligible for harm.

The Real Harm

Current legal remedies may be missing the real harm of racist indoctrination, which may not be immediately apparent or verifiable. For instance, hate expressions tend to encourage a set of beliefs that develop gradually and that often can lie dormant until conditions are ripe for a climate of moral exclusion and subsequent crimes against humanity. Moral exclusion is defined by Susan Opotow, an independent scholar affiliated with Teachers College at Columbia University, as the psychosocial orientation toward individuals or groups for whom justice principles or considerations of fairness are not applicable. People who are morally excluded are perceived as nonentities, and harming them appears acceptable and just (e.g., slavery, holocaust).

It is not the abstract viewpoints that are problematic. Rather, it is the expressions intending to elicit persecution or oppression that often begin with dehumanizing rhetoric. In my research, I argue that communication is the primary means by which psychological distancing occurs. Arguably, it may be the long-term, not short-term, effects of hate expression that are potentially more far reaching.

Examining the Internet

Even though prevailing First Amendment dogma maintains that speech may not be penalized merely because its content is racist, sexist or basically abhorrent, Internet law is a dynamic area and as such is not completely integrated into our regulatory and legal system. Consequently, many questions remain about how traditional laws should apply to this new and unique medium.

The Internet can combine elements of print (newspapers and magazines), broadcast (television and radio) and face-to-face interaction. Moreover, unlike users of previous media, those on the Internet have the power to reach a mass audience, but in this case the audience must be more active in seeking information, as cyberspace is less intrusive than other mass media.

It is unclear whether content-based restrictions found in other technological media may be permissible for the Internet.

For example, the FCC [Federal Communications Commission] ruled that indecency was unsuitable for broadcast media because of ease of access, invasiveness and spectrum scarcity, yet cable and print media are not subjected to this form of content regulation.

In 1996, the United States Congress passed the Telecommunications Bill, which included the Communications Decency Act (CDA). The CDA regulated indecent or obscene material for adults on the Internet, applying First Amendment jurisprudence from broadcast and obscenity cases. Later that year, the Supreme Court declared two provisions unconstitutional in *Reno vs. American Civil Liberties Union*. Congress and the Court disagreed on the medium-specific constitutional speech standard suitable for the World Wide Web. Congress argued that the Internet should be regulated in the same manner as television or radio, but the Court decided not to apply that doctrinal framework. Instead, the Court viewed the Internet as face-to-face communication, deserving full protection.

Is Regulation Possible?

Issues of Internet regulation naturally lead to the question of whether such regulation is even possible. Cyberspace doesn't have geographical boundaries, so it is difficult to determine where violations of the law should be prosecuted. There are enforcement conflicts, not only between different countries' legal jurisdictions, but also among federal, state and local levels in the United States. Although Americans place a high premium on free expression, without much effort most people can find Internet material that they would want to censor.

Some argue that cyberhate oversteps this idea of "mere insult" and warrants liability. The Internet is a powerful forum of communication with its broad (world-wide) reach, interactivity and multi-media capability to disseminate information. These features inevitably result in concerns about impact, es-

Exceptions to the First Amendment

Rules against hate speech, homophobic remarks and misogyny serve both symbolic and institutional values—increasing productivity in the workplace and protecting a learning environment on campus. It has been argued that such prohibitions operate in derogation of the First Amendment's guarantee of freedom of speech, but that amendment already is subject to dozens of exceptions—libel, defamation, words of conspiracy or threat, disrespectful words uttered to a judge or police officer, irrelevant or untrue words spoken in a judicial proceeding, copyright, plagiarism, official secrets, misleading advertising and many more. The social interest in deterring vicious racial or sexual vituperation certainly seems at least as great as that underlying these other forms of speech deemed unworthy of First Amendment protection.

Richard Delgado, Insight on the News, *June 24, 1996.*

pecially when viewed as empowering racists and other extremists. It is common for people to wonder whether white supremacist Web pages cause hate crime. This question is similar to people's concerns regarding whether TV violence causes aggression in viewers. The issue of causation (claim: x causes y) is an important one to address.

It is important to differentiate between language determining (or causing) an effect and language influencing the probability of an effect. In terms of a strict social science approach (deterministic causation) we can't say language has an effect unless three conditions are met: (a) there must be a relationship between the hypothesized cause and the observed effect, (b) the cause must always precede the effect in time (x must come before y), and (c) all alternative explanations for the effect must be eliminated. The problem with making a strong case for a causal effect lies with the second and third conditions. For example, most media (television, Internet, etc.) effects are probabilistic, not deterministic. It is almost impossible to make a clear case for television or cyberhate effects because the relationship is almost never a simple causal one. Instead, there are many factors in the influence process. Each factor increases the probability of an effect occurring. The effects process is complex.

The U.S. Supreme Court has traditionally viewed speech effects in terms of short-term, deterministic consequences, and has not considered more far-reaching effects.

While more research is needed on the long-term effects of hate speech, it may be worth considering some very limited restrictions on some hate expression. American jurisprudence has not fully realized the harmful nature and effects stemming from hate speech, which has the ability both to directly elicit immediate behavior (short term) and to cultivate an oppressive climate (long term).

| "Hate speech is the very essence of free speech."

Hate Speech Should Not Be Regulated

Ted Gup

Ted Gup, a journalism professor at Case Western Reserve University in Cleveland, Ohio, argues in the following viewpoint that free expression of hate speech is essential to reducing bigotry in society. He contends that hatred and racism flourish when open debate is discouraged. Allowing open discussion of hateful ideas is the best way to invite opposing voices that discredit prejudice and encourage tolerance, in the author's opinion.

As you read, consider the following questions:

1. What incident clarified the difference between speech and action for the author?

2. As quoted by Ted Gup, what is Abe Ayad's goal?

3. According to Gup, what reaction do symbols of hate elicit in society?

Ted Gup, "At the Corner of Hate and Free Speech," *Washington Post*, December 15, 2002, p. B1. Reproduced by permission of the author.

I would like to have lunch at Grandpa's Kitchen, a convenience store and deli on East 55th and Chester [in Cleveland, Ohio]. But despite its warm and fuzzy name, I fear that I would not be entirely welcome there. I say this because of the huge mural on the side of the building that depicts Jews as monkeys wearing yarmulkes. The owner, a Mr. Brahim "Abe" Ayad, has made it pretty clear that he is none too fond of people of my faith. He has his reasons, many of them involving his father, a Palestinian who he says was driven from his land to make way for the state of Israel. Today, Grandpa's Kitchen is a kind of local landmark, a testament to unmuzzled anti-Semitism. But the fact that this animosity has been allowed to fester publicly is one that I, the grandson of a rabbi, applaud without reservation.

I am drawn to Grandpa's Kitchen because it is contested ground between those who argue that they have a right to be rid of such venomous expression and those who say it is a vital exercise of free speech. It is a debate being carried on not only on this seedy Cleveland corner but also by the Supreme Court, which [in 2002] heard arguments on whether cross burning should be considered protected free speech.[1]

Even Harvard Law School, where generations of students have been trained to defend the First Amendment, [considered] a speech code targeted at the lexicon of hate [in 2002]. In this it is hardly alone. Corporations, clubs, elementary schools and universities have convinced themselves that the enlightened thing to do is to declare that "Hate speech is not free speech," to quote Robert A. Corrigan, the president of San Francisco State University.

I believe they are not only wrong but dangerously wrong. Any effort to stifle hate speech is a betrayal of democratic val-

---

1. In *Virginia v. Black* in 2002, the Supreme Court decided that states could lawfully ban the burning of crosses as a means of intimidation or harassment. The case was brought by two men, Richard J. Elliott and Jonathan O'Mara, who were convicted by Virginia law of setting fire to a cross in an African American man's yard. A state court overturned the verdict, but the Supreme Court reversed the decision, upholding the Virginia law.

ues—the very ones that ultimately protect diversity and dissent. It seems to me that unfettered speech is to bigotry what a vaccine is to smallpox.

Sticks and Stones

I understand the emotional appeal of speech codes, and I well know how noxious and hurtful words can be. As a Jew growing up in Ohio in the 1950s, I was branded a "shylock" and a "kike." I was threatened and, on occasion, beaten. In junior high, two classmates stabbed me with a pencil, and four decades later, two graphite points are still plainly visible in my left hand. That helped clarify for me the difference between speech and action, or the "sticks and stones" rule of the playground. Today my sons, adopted from South Korea, also know that words can be ugly. I listen in pained silence as they tell me of classmates who taunt them by pinching the corners of their own eyes or call them "chinks." Over a soda, I tell my son who gets off the yellow school bus with a black eye that I understand, even if I can't explain what fuels his tormenters.

But as a journalist and as an American, I feel a curious, almost perverse, sense of pride that Grandpa's Kitchen, with its notorious mural, could find a secure place in this city of immigrants and minorities. Beyond that, I have a feeling that Abe (as I have begun to think of him) may have something to teach me and that I owe him—no, I owe myself—a visit. And so I call him at the deli, identify myself as both a journalist and a Jew, and ask if his door is open to me. "I'm open to all good people," he says with such warmth that I am left almost speechless. "Thanks," I hear myself say. "Look forward to meeting you." (Did I really say that?) "All right, brother," he says. Brother?

On a scrap of paper, I jot down—"Monday/Lunch/Grandpa's Kitchen"—as if I might forget.

By permission Asay and Creators Syndicate, Inc.

The first thing I see as I pull up to the deli is the mural, a pastiche of offensive images and accusations. One depicts a Jewish conspiracy in control of American network television. Another shows Jesus Christ in agony on the cross. Just inside the door, a news article is tacked to the wall: "Tel Aviv Mayor Seeks Help in Cleveland." Above it is written "Proof Implicating Jews." Am I not now in hostile territory?

I have a pretty good idea of what Abe will be like—crude, mean-spirited, not too smart. But the man well-known for the past several years for his offensive murals approaches me in a white apron and extends a huge hand. He is courtly, soft-spoken and oddly vulnerable. He offers me a cup of coffee and puts a fresh pot on to brew. At 36, he is a big man, 6-foot-1, 250 pounds. His eyes are hidden behind gold-rimmed sunglasses. He seems as curious about me as I am about him. There are no tables or chairs, only a takeout counter, so he stacks plastic milk crates in the aisle should we want to sit.

Challenging Stereotypes

I had expected someone consumed with hate and at first he confirms my stereotype. He hands me a book entitled "The Ugly Truth About the ADL [Anti-Defamation League]." He calls [the terrorist attacks on September 11, 2001] a Jewish conspiracy and produces a poster depicting Israeli leaders astride missiles labeled "Nuke" and "Chemical." Their target is spelled out: "Islam World or Bust."

But if he is a bigot he is most selective. A moment earlier, the poster was hidden behind a painting celebrating Black History Month, a work done at his expense and featuring Malcolm X and Jesse Jackson and others. Elsewhere are certificates recording his contributions to a Baptist church (he is a Muslim), to George Washington Carver Elementary and to an organization for foster children. Maybe, I tell myself, he's just a shrewd businessman ingratiating himself with the African American community. But he seems so earnest. Most of his patrons are black, and he greets them with a hug and calls them "Brother."

His menu also reflects a certain ecumenicalism: gyros, Polish Boy sausages, catfish and okra, and a Reuben (what Jewish deli would be without?).

I have come to find out who Abe is and what he wants. The answer to each is the same. He is the son of a Palestinian who immigrated to the United States in 1926 and whose service to the U.S. Army in World War II left him disabled, he says.

Abe was born in Dearborn, Mich. At 6, he and his family moved back to the West Bank. At 8, he says, he was on his way to school when an Israeli soldier shot him with a rubber bullet. At my request, he rolls up his pant leg to show me the dime-sized scar on his knee. He says he was also shot in the rump. We both laugh as he declines to proffer the evidence. That same day, he says, two of his friends were shot dead.

"How do you like your coffee?" he asks.

What is it, I ask him, that he hopes to accomplish with his attacks on Jews? "It should be perceived as a plea for help," he says. "I'm not going to hurt anybody. That is not even an option." He adds, "I just want to vent my frustrations and my disappointments. How else could I get their attention?" And then there is his quixotic effort to win back lands he says were his father's and are his rightful inheritance, land on which, he says, there are now Jewish settlements and factories. "ALL I WANT IS MY LAND" is painted on the mural. "I just want justice. I can't ask for revenge—that's God's. I'm just trying to break the cycle of hate that's been consuming us."

But how can he expect to promote understanding while using words of hate? How misguided, I think. He is also critical of the Palestinian government and suicide bombers. "We're at fault just as much because we're targeting innocent people," he says. Hurting anyone is "the last thing I'm trying to do."

He is a father of eight. I ask him what lessons he teaches his children. "I tell them to stand up for what's right. Don't let anybody step on anybody and don't step on anybody. You don't have to be afraid of anybody. Not here. Never here." Not so different from what I tell my own sons.

Hidden Prejudice

The landscape of my youth had no such murals of intolerance. Instead, prejudice was hidden behind disingenuous smiles and behind the manicured hedges of off-limits country clubs and the ivied walls of universities with secret quotas. As a boy in Canton, Ohio, I remember my family fantasized about living beside a lake on the edge of town, but we knew it was closed to "our kind." The word that was used, if it was uttered at all, was "restricted." How antiseptic.

The year Abe was born, I was attending a Midwest boarding school where I suffered overt anti-Semitism from some of my classmates. But I also suspected that the school itself was complicit. I felt unwelcome and inadequate. For years, I wondered whether I was just paranoid. Then, two decades after graduation, I was invited to return as a "distinguished" guest-lecturer. That was when I got a glimpse of my student file. There, on the outside jacket, was a Star of David and a tiny notation that suggested that perhaps in the future, local fathers might screen out such applicants.

The note didn't upset me as much as it brought a sense of relief that my suspicions were being confirmed. If only I and others of my generation had had the opportunity to confront the authors of such notes. If only they had spoken their objections and aired their biases publicly. Why in the world would we now, in the name of speech codes, want to drive them back into the safety of their secret lairs?

Speech codes threaten to take us back to the old days when prejudice was vented only in whispers between like minds. My own history has convinced me that a silenced bigot can do far more mischief than one who airs his hatred publicly.

The Best Defense

From my parents I learned the difference between the acute sting of an ethnic slur and the anguish of a polite cold shoulder. Years ago, a clerk at a fashionable Virginia Beach hotel discreetly asked my parents about our family name, then turned them away into the night. They were on their honeymoon. That was 1947, the year the movie *Gentleman's Agreement* captured the silent complicity upon which anti-Semitism—indeed all bigotry—depends. The other evening I lent the film to an African American neighbor. He returned it the next morning shaking his head and told me about his own experience. Working through a team of lawyers, only weeks before he had been close to buying a company. Then the owners discovered he was black. The price tripled. The deal fell through. Nothing uncivil was ever said, but it seldom is. That's why I defend Abe's right to express his hostilities. I see it as my own best defense.

Don't get me wrong. The murals make me cringe, but I much prefer that his feelings be out in the open. They tell me where I stand with Abe. They also invite the possibility, however slim, that we might find some sliver of common ground, that confrontation could lead to conciliation.

Even the most reviled of hate symbols, the burning cross and the swastika, are just that—emblems of unspeakable evil. But their sporadic resurfacing has produced not waves of terror but waves of public revulsion, not Kristallnachts[2] and lynchings but community rallies against racism. Hate speech need not be a precursor to violence. On the contrary, it can defuse tensions that could turn explosive. Hate speech can discredit nascent movements that might otherwise draw strength from authoritarian efforts to snuff them out. Intimidation invites intimidation.

Speech codes empower the impotent. I wince when I hear raw ethnic, racial and sexual slurs. But even worse is the notion that people who think that way could move about among us, unknown and unchallenged. "You can't cure it if you can't hear it," my mother says. She's right. Bigotry is an affliction not of the mouth but of the mind.

And while free speech often causes pain, it also holds out the only real promise of progress. In the end, like it or not, hate speech is the very essence of free speech and its airing is and always has been a potent self-corrective. This is what Abe may be able to teach Harvard Law.

Opening a Dialogue

I have no illusion that my visit with Abe changed his mind about Jews or put out years of smoldering resentment, but it did open a dialogue and, humble as that may be, it is a start. Not long before, a . . . columnist, Regina Brett, did something similar by suggesting a new use for a billboard next to

---

2. *Kristallnacht*, meaning the "night of broken glass," is the name given to acts of vandalism by Nazi youths committed against Jewish property on a night in Vienna in 1939.

Grandpa's Kitchen. Today, in red letters two feet high it declares: "The Hate Stops Here." It may be an opening salvo. The feelings Abe has stirred have triggered something larger—a community campaign against bigotry.

I ask him what he thinks of the sign, expecting him to denounce it. "'The Hate Stops Here.' I hope it does." He adds proudly, "That's my sign. That's my message. I mean look at what one man can do—me." Once more he's left me speechless. "Let's make sure the hate stops here," he says, "and not just sweep it under the rug. Let's resolve it like human beings."

Well, maybe the hate doesn't quite stop here—not yet anyway, but maybe someday.

*"Without a measure of legal protection
the flag is devalued . . . and destined to
disappear."*

Flag Desecration Should
Be Restricted

Shawntel Smith

*In the following viewpoint, Shawntel Smith attempts to persuade
Congress to enact an amendment that would protect the American flag from desecration. She contends that the flag symbolizes
the values that make America great: freedom, opportunity, and
unity. Desecrating the flag, she argues, essentially rejects the values that the flag represents. The proposed amendment was defeated in 1999. Smith is a former Miss America winner.*

As you read, consider the following questions:

1. What is the "American dream," as defined by the author?

2. In Shawntel Smith's opinion, why is the American flag
   unique?

3. According to Smith, why is desecrating the flag not protected as free speech?

Shawntel Smith, testimony before the U.S. House of Representatives, Washington, DC,
March 23, 1999.

Mr. Chairman, members of the House Judiciary Sub-committee, my name is Shawntel Smith and I proudly call Muldrow, Oklahoma my home. It is an honor to speak to each of you today in support of House Joint Resolution 33, a proposed constitutional amendment that would restore the Flag of the United States of America to its proper place of honor.[1]

I, like many others, have had family members serve in the military. They served very courageously and proudly. Just to name a few, my Great-grandfather Powell served in the Civil War. My Grandfather Fouts—Roy Gideon Fouts—served as Seaman First Class in World War II. My Grandpa Smith—Harold Elmo Smith—served as a supply Sergeant in World War II and was on one of the first waves onto the beaches of Normandy. And my father Gailen Maurice Smith served as a Sergeant in the National Guard. I have great pride that my family has contributed to preserving the freedoms that our great nation stands for, and the symbol of that freedom, the United States Flag.

The American Dream

I count myself fortunate as one of but a few American women to have conferred upon them the tide of "Miss America." As the 75th Miss America, I traveled some 20,000 miles a month sharing the message of STW [School-To-Work] Reinventing America's Work Force. I visited 48 states and encouraged young people to develop skills, set goals, dream dreams and to become all they wish to become. I continue to share this message as ambassador for the U.S. Departments of Education and Labor. I also share with young people that life is not about fairy tales but that it is about never giving up, never giving in and overcoming obstacles that may arise. I believe in the American Dream—which is the freedom to achieve greatness through hard work, perseverance and determination.

1. The proposed flag desecration amendment was defeated in the Senate.

I believe, as I stated earlier, that our flag is the symbol of the American Dream. I can remember standing in elementary school and saying the Pledge of Allegiance. And, today, I love watching the little boy or girl reciting the Pledge of Allegiance at the top of their lungs. Young people that say the Pledge of Allegiance with such boldness view the flag as a cornerstone—one of strength, safety and opportunity. I am constantly amazed at the reverence it receives from our youngest Americans. Children exhibit special concern . . . to treat it reverently, to stand tall and proud as they recite the Pledge of Allegiance.

It was brought to my attention not too long ago, indeed, most Americans would be shocked to learn that today it is okay, not illegal, to desecrate the symbol of our nation, the symbol of hope for the world's people—the American Flag. In fact [of] those who were informed about the current law, or lack of a protecting law, 80% favored an amendment to the constitution that would provide legal protection of Old Glory.

Restoring the Star Spangled Banner

Not far from Capitol Hill, in the Museum of American History, a project is underway to restore the Star Spangled Banner, the 15-star, 15-stripe flag that is THE symbol of determination for a free people. It is one flag around which our nation now begins to rally in order to preserve and protect us as we move into the new millennium. Part of a government program to preserve national treasures, more than $5 million will be dedicated to its preservation.

There are two interesting points, among many, about this particular flag: It is the largest historic textile in the world, and is one of invaluable historic significance. In short, it is a piece of cloth that reminds us of our heritage—as is, as does, every American Flag.

We might ask: Is the Star Spangled Banner of 1814 THE flag of the United States? Yes and No. There were other similar

Justifiable Limitations on the First Amendment

Many well-meaning folks contend that if we prohibit the desecration of our flag, we do harm to our right to free speech secured by the First Amendment. While I understand these feelings, I disagree with them. I do not believe that the burning or desecration of our flag constitutes speech. It is conduct. As such, the First Amendment has no application to flag desecration, because the First Amendment protects only speech.

Even if flag burning and the like could be considered a form of speech, the First Amendment should not reach this manner of speech. The First Amendment is not absolute. For instance, there is no First Amendment right to yell fire in a theater or to provoke others through fighting words. The flag occupies such a critical, unique place in our nation's life that its desecration amounts to "fighting words" for many. For the reasons I set forth above, I believe that another justifiable limitation on the First Amendment is the protection of our national symbol, Old Glory.

John N. Hostettler, "Position on a Constitutional Amendment Prohibiting Flag Desecration," July 3, 2002.

flags before, and many others that came later, each of which [was] and still [is] THE flag of the United States.

Some might argue that burning "A" flag is different from burning "THE" flag of 1814. Our flag, however, is unique in that it exists only in copies and, therefore, every flag is THE flag. If we recognize the need to preserve and protect the Star Spangled Banner, then we should recognize the value and need in the preservation and protection of all Star Spangled Banners.

The Star Spangled Banner in the museum is, physically, less than the one we might envision. Over the years, well meaning Americans have clipped portions off as souvenirs, or awards, with no regard to the importance of keeping the flag whole. Had his practice gone unchecked, the Star Spangled Banner would be but a memory.

Those who oppose legal protection, well meaning as they may be, relegate the flag of the United States to the same fate. Without a measure of legal protection the flag is devalued, figuratively "clipped" and destined to disappear.

Embodying America

The flag of the United States flies today as it did over Fort McHenry. And today, just as it did then, it embodies what we think of as America and it causes us to pause and remember what and who got us here.

The memory of Americans who gave their lives is woven in every stitch of the flag, no matter its size or age. And, whether it flew over Fort McHenry, over the US Capitol, or from the hand of a young child, the integrity of the flag of the United States deserves protection and preservation.

As we go to the millennium, we are looking back on our heritage with a deep concern for preserving those things uniquely American. The 106th Congress has the opportunity to be part of this preservation effort by providing our flag a measure of protection from desecration.

While the archives at the Museum mark the millennium by saving crumbling pieces of our heritage that are in danger of being lost, a flag protection amendment could do the same. It can limit the destructive actions of those who would literally rip the flag apart, causing it to crumble and committing it to history, ultimately lost as a "living" symbol of our great nation.

A Values Issue

Burning a flag is not a matter of free speech, but I believe it is a matter of behavior. It is an insult to the intelligence of the vast majority of common-sense Americans to call flag burning "speech." This is a values issue for the American people. America is a tapestry of diverse peoples. The uniqueness of our nation is our diversity. The flag represents the values, traditions and aspirations that bind us together as a nation. It stands above our differences and unites us in war and peace.

Because I was blessed with the position of Miss America, I had many unforgettable experiences. One in particular I would like to share with you today. Just after beginning my year of service I was asked by the governor of Oklahoma, Governor Frank Keating, to participate in the Thank You America Tour—which gave thanks to all of those who so generously and bravely helped during the 1995 Oklahoma City bombing.[2] Being from Oklahoma I took great pride and felt such honor to participate in the ceremony at our nation's capital, Washington, D.C. I remember walking into the war memorial room in which the ceremony was held; I was overwhelmed with emotion not only for the reason we were there but also because of what I saw. As I looked across the room, I saw flags from all the different countries and in the center of the room, there was a large United States flag. At that moment, I thought of all the men and women who fought for our country, many even sacrificed their lives. I was also reminded of how in a time of crisis we as Americans pull together to help one another.

I thank you for the opportunity to be here today and to share my concern for protecting the flag of the United States. I hope to have conveyed to you a few of the many meanings the United States flag embodies. Meanings of freedom, the

---

2. In 1995 Timothy McVeigh bombed the Oklahoma City Federal Building, killing 168 people and injuring more than five hundred.

American Dream, strength, security, opportunity, heritage and unity. To desecrate the flag would be to desecrate all that the flag stands for.

> "To forbid flag burning is to forbid you from disposing of your property in ways that offend others."

Flag Desecration Should Not Be Restricted

Andrew Cohen

According to Andrew Cohen in the following viewpoint, legislation prohibiting flag burning is unconstitutional. He contends that there is no one "American flag," but rather only individually owned flags. Since flags are property, and because property rights are constitutionally protected, flag owners may burn their flags with impunity. The values that the flag symbolizes—self-determination and freedom from oppression—are not harmed by someone desecrating his or her own property, in Cohen's opinion. Cohen teaches philosophy at the University of Wisconsin, Stevens Point.

As you read, consider the following questions:

1. What does freedom of speech guarantee, according to the author?

Andrew Cohen, "Flags, Flames, and Property," *Freeman*, vol. 49, January 1999, pp. 24–26. Copyright © 1999 Foundation for Economic Education, Incorporated, www.fee.org. All rights reserved.

2. When is the one time burning a flag should be against the law, in the author's opinion?

3. According to Andrew Cohen, for what did members of the armed services fight?

A constitutional amendment that would forbid the desecration of American flags is again percolating in the nation's capital.[1] As of this writing [1999], the immediate prospects for passage look bleak. But this amendment has a way of never fully going away. Many opponents of the measure trot out free speech arguments. And although concerns about free expression are important, these traditional arguments miss a more central political principle that the amendment and resulting laws against flag burning would jeopardize: property rights. The amendment would undermine key liberties for which the flag stands.

Arguments for Flag Desecration Laws

Those who uphold laws against flag desecration typically speak of the important values that the flag symbolizes. They claim that legally allowing flag burning is tantamount to rejecting the freedoms that the flag represents. They say it is vital that we express our respect for human freedom by institutionalizing penalties against those who would defile the national symbol.

Permitting flag burning, the amendment's proponents continue, sends the wrong message to America's youth, America's voters, and observers abroad. When the young see protesters publicly burning a flag with impunity, they may believe that American freedoms are cheap. They may then think that the nation's commitment to uphold those freedoms is fleeting. Permitting flag burning may also undermine a key basis for community among America's voters. With protesters burning flags, voters may lose a vision of shared citizenship and be less

1. The proposed flag desecration amendment was defeated in 1999 in the Senate.

committed to the American ideal. Flag burning is also supposedly a slap in the face to all Americans who suffered in wartime to secure freedoms for everyone. Lastly, foreign observers who see Americans burning their own flag may be less inclined to support America's international policies aimed at securing freedom. Advocates fear that foreigners will think: if Americans cannot take their own freedoms seriously, then we need not take seriously the moral reasoning they present to the world.

The Free Speech Argument Against Flag Desecration Laws

People who burn flags intend to send a message by doing so. This is what makes flag burning a form of expression. Some flag burners take offense at various American foreign policy measures. (Recall the nightly news broadcast [in 1998] showing Sudanese burning American flags in Khartoum after the United States bombed what it deemed a suspicious pharmaceutical factory.) Some individuals may burn flags as a way of saying America is not true to its own values. Others simply despise American ideals and set the flag aflame. In any case, people who burn flags do so deliberately in order to send a public message of protest.

The First Amendment to the Constitution reads, "Congress shall make no law . . . abridging the freedom of speech." Constitutional scholars and legal theorists have long argued over the meaning of this amendment. There is, however, a rough consensus on two ideas: (1) the amendment protects peaceful expression, popular or unpopular, but (2) the framers clearly did not intend for it to license any and all forms of expression. Consequently, room has been made for laws against libel, slander, and obscenity. Contrary to hyperbolic op-eds railing against flaming protests, burning a flag is not "obscene." At worst, it is despicable. At best, it is a valuable form of political speech.

The First Amendment protects freedom of speech, which in turn protects the liberty to say wrong-headed, bigoted, stupid, vicious things. Such protection is crucial; otherwise freedom of speech would reduce to the empty freedom to say only the right, the true, and the good. That would present a disturbing practical difficulty: Some bureaucrat would have to decide what is permissible speech, because in today's pluralistic society, there is little consensus on many aspects of the right, the true, and the good. Freedom of speech, however, is the freedom to say what one wishes without having to solicit the permission of anyone first.

Freedom of speech guarantees a healthy, open marketplace of ideas. More fundamentally, it includes the freedom to say things that others might not like. Those who are offended should respond with reasoned arguments of their own and not by passing a law. If individuals were only free to say things that others liked, public and private discussions would be banal, stilted, and oppressed. A law against flag burning forbids a form of expression simply because others do not like the message. Government exists, however, to protect individual rights. It should not protect citizens from being offended. We can stipulate that many acts of flag burning are offensive. Simply being offensive, however, does not violate individual rights.

The Property Rights Argument Against Flag Burning

The free speech argument against the proposed amendment is powerful; people must be free to offend if free speech is to count for anything. There is, however, one time when flag burning should be against the law: when it's someone else's flag.

Suppose you own a flag. Suppose that Chris takes your flag without your consent and sets it on fire in the public square. What Chris has done ought to be forbidden (and

The Rights of American Citizens

Banning flag desecration is an obvious and serious breach of the First Amendment and speech freedoms. We haven't seen protesters burning flags for the fun of it. When someone does this, they are making a serious political statement, which is, lo and behold, a guaranteed right of every U.S. citizen.

Anonymous,
Orange County Register, *July 23, 2001.*

punished) not because he burned a flag, but because he burned your flag. Chris ought to be held accountable just as if he had taken a sledgehammer to your concrete garden gnomes without your permission. He destroyed your property.

People who debate the flag issue often lose sight of this important fact: You cannot burn "the American flag" because there is no such thing as "the American flag." There are only flags. The "American flag" is an idea that cannot be burned. A particular flag, however, can be burned. Whether it is permissible to do so turns on whose flag it is.

Being a material object, a flag usually comes into the world attached to someone as property. A law against flag burning would forbid you from disposing of your property as you see fit. Let us assume that burning your flag does not pose a threat to public safety (that is, you don't ignite and toss it into an unsuspecting crowd). In that case, when you burn your flag, your actions are not importantly different from taking your paper and your ink to print up pamphlets that say anything (or even nothing) at all. The pamphlets are your property, and so too is your flag. Passersby can take your message or leave it.

To forbid flag burning is to forbid you from disposing of your property in ways that offend others. But property rights protect freedom of action for which one need not solicit the permission of others. A right to your flag guarantees a right to burn it, stomp on it, spit on it, or turn it into underwear if you so choose. Your flag is your property. If someone does not like what you do with your property, he should not lock you up; he should persuade you to change your ways or he should have nothing to do with you. Consider the absurdity of having rights to use your property only in ways others find acceptable.

Permissible Flag Burning and Some Problems

When a flag becomes old and tattered, there is a prescribed way to dispose of it. Part of the process involves burning it. If flag burning were forbidden, presumably it would not be just any flag burning that would be illegal. It would only be flag-burning-while-thinking-nasty-thoughts-about-the-flag. If persons are to be punished not for what they do, but for what they think, we will have marched a long way from the freedoms on which this nation was founded, and headed dangerously closer to tyranny.

There are further difficulties with laws against flag burning. We all know what an American flag is supposed to look like. It has 50 stars and 13 stripes, all arranged in a certain pattern. Suppose, however, you were to sew a piece of fabric that looked just like a current American flag, except that it had 49 stars or 50 six-sided stars (instead of five-sided stars), or white stripes on the very top and very bottom (instead of red), or a blue field that was only six stripes high (instead of seven). Strictly speaking, those pieces of fabric would not be American flags. They would be imperfect approximations of American flags. Would a law against flag burning forbid the desecration of any piece of fabric that even looked like an

American flag? What if one takes a big piece of white paper and writes in big boldface letters, "THIS IS AN AMERICAN FLAG," and sets it on fire? Perhaps the courts would rule that any act intended to make onlookers believe that one was burning an American flag would be covered by the amendment. Once again, however, the government would be getting into the business of punishing people for having bad thoughts. This is not the mark of a government in a free society.

What the Flag Means

The flag is a symbol of American values such as self-determination and freedom from oppression. Throughout our history, members of the armed services suffered on behalf of freedom, not on behalf of a piece of fabric. They did not put their lives on the line so that busybodies and bureaucrats could tell us what we can or cannot say and what we can or cannot do with our property.

No doubt, flag burners are often quite vicious, detestable persons whose contempt for American values deserves our contempt. But the law should not forbid all vicious conduct. We can privately refuse to have anything to do with such persons. We can hold them up to public scorn. We might display our patriotism to counter the flag-burning demonstration. Such acts would help solidify the shared citizenship that flag-burning amendment advocates so often invoke. Those informal responses would also help send the message that some matters are best left to private individuals and the free choices they make. Those who take freedom seriously are civilized enough to put flag burners in their place without beating them up or locking them up.

Supporters of laws to punish people who destroy a flag betray their belief that the values the flag symbolizes cannot prevail on their own merits. They seem to think that freedom demands government-mandated respect. But American ideals are sturdy enough to await voluntary respect. Let us repudiate flag burners and persuade (not force) individuals to respect the flag. We must not, however, cheapen the freedoms the flag represents with an amendment that would restrict individual rights.

"Images of real and virtual child porn
... are indistinguishable."

Virtual Child Pornography Should Be Banned

Paul M. Rodriguez

In the following viewpoint, Paul M. Rodriguez argues that virtual child pornography—computer-generated depictions of children engaged in sex acts—is as dangerous to children as pornography that depicts actual children. He contends that these pictures are indistinguishable from photographs and video of real children and may excite predators to molest young children. The government should enact legislation that would outlaw virtual child pornography, in Rodriguez's opinion. In April 2003 Congress passed legislation that tightened restrictions on real and virtual child pornography and strengthened penalties for repeat offenders. Rodriguez is the managing editor of Insight on the News, *a biweekly newsmagazine.*

As you read, consider the following questions:

1. According to the author, in what important ways is adult pornography different from child pornography?

2. Why did pornographers post pictures of normal children on their Web sites, according to Paul M. Rodriguez?

3. What suggestions does Rodriguez offer to reduce the spread of virtual child pornography?

Researching our story about the 2002 Supreme Court decision approving "virtual" child pornography, we wanted to present a visual image that would bring home the horror of this outrage.[1] After extensive calls to the top photo sources failed to produce anything that approximated actual photography of the kind still banned by law, we turned to the Internet. Brother, what a shock it was to see what's out there on the World Wide Web. And we don't mean just every imaginable (or unimaginable) version of hard-core porn, but even the innocent listings that often are attached to pornographic materials.

Equally disturbing (and we'll explain this further on) were porn links that led through images and virtual graphics that seemed not to be pornography at all. In fact, a number of such "binary" sites we found with the help of savvy Webmasters were shocking because they began with the kind of harmless photographs and images of children that might be found in school yearbooks, family albums or Sunday school bulletins.

The importance of the apparently innocent pictures is, in fact, at the core of our laws against child porn, and it eviscerates the Supreme Court's extraordinarily stupid decision that says virtual images of children used as sexual props is okay because no crime against real children is involved and so publication is protected by the First Amendment.

1. In *Ashcroft v. Free Speech Coalition* in 2002, the Supreme Court decided that the First Amendment protects pornography or other sexual images that only appear to depict real children engaged in sex.

Endangering Children

Pornography involving consenting adults invokes far different issues than child porn. Our society long ago distinguished the dramatic differences between the two and decided that the latter is aberrant, deviant, depraved and immoral. It endangers the safety of innocent children, which is why it is illegal. It harms children who are exploited foully to make it and it provides a potential catalyst for pederasts and other sexual perverts who may go from images to the real thing—a crime in which victims often are psychologically crippled or even murdered to ensure their silence. Society simply decided that the risk of child rape being excited by this stuff is too great to be tolerated.

Indeed, laws against child pornography are designed to accomplish two things: 1) protect children from exploitation for its production and 2) create firewalls to prevent such material from being obtained by wannabe, in-waiting or impulse-driven child-sex predators who the courts, law enforcement, victims and even the criminals themselves claim are excited to act out their loathsome fantasies by pornographic images of children. The medical profession long has believed that those convicted of child-sex abuse are unlikely ever to be cured of their "illness." Some penologists claim there literally is a 100 percent recidivism rate for pederasts.

Which brings us back to those seemingly innocent photographs and images of children on the Internet. It puzzled us, so we followed an escalating trail of pornographic links with headers such as "virtual porn," "child porn" and similar variations. Not only were the pornographers baiting a virtual path to their hard-core sites with images of innocence, but whoever did this understood that their pederast clientele wants to pursue child sex by sorting through pictures of normal children. The search for the victim is part of the perversion that drives some to harm children.

Unless the government case was completely incompetent, the Supreme Court should have known all of this, yet it ignored the prevention aspects of the law against virtual child porn that it struck down. In doing this the court brazenly and irresponsibly dismissed an essential ingredient of that law: recognition of the effects even virtual child porn has on encouraging potential child molesters.

Indistinguishable from Real Children

In conversations with some of the leading entrepreneurs of virtual technology we learned something else that the apparently ignorant Supreme Court majority overlooked. The industry already can create human images indistinguishable from images of real people and can animate them to do anything at all. Virtual reality is just that—images of computer-generated humans made to act in any way their creators wish them to behave. Check out the image from *Final Fantasy: The Spirit Within.* . . . The virtual girl appears real in every way. The same thing is being done pornographically, we're told, with virtual children engaging in sexual acts—children indistinguishable from real children to the pederasts, whetting their appetites for molestation.

Indeed, we're told by medical and law-enforcement experts, molesters excited by child porn who attack children don't give a damn whether it is real or virtual when the one is indistinguishable from the other. Unfortunately, in its rush to judgment, the liberal majority that now dominates the Supreme Court failed to see the bigger picture. For that matter, it failed even to see the images of real and virtual child porn that are indistinguishable.

Congress and the Bush administration are working to overcome the high court's blunder. Perhaps part of that effort ought to include a cyber-warfare agency that employs the military or intelligence technology now used to hunt down terrorists via the Internet. It should be a relatively simple mat-

Feeding the Market

Lack of resources, ever-changing technology, and the free flow of information over the Internet have compounded the already daunting responsibility of law enforcement to eliminate child pornography. Use of computer technology to commit child pornography offenses is at an all-time high. Federal prosecutions of Internet child pornographers have increased by 10 percent every year since 1995, with over 400 cases prosecuted each year in the federal courts alone. Offenders can view and trade child pornography while sitting in the comfort of their homes, an especially attractive option for avoiding detection. Digital technology has enhanced the quality of images available and increased the volume of information that can be accessed. Scanners and inexpensive software packages now allow offenders to create virtual child pornography, which they often trade for more explicit images of real children. The invention of Web cameras even allows individuals to molest children in "real time," while others watch from their homes over the Internet. Child pornographers are always seeking more, and more explicit, child pornography. Virtual child pornography feeds this cycle and sustains the market. As technology continues to become cheaper and more advanced, the volume of child pornography being traded over the Internet will rise exponentially.

Daniel S. Armagh,
Cardozo Law Review, *October 20, 2002.*

ter to apply existing child-porn standards against the international child-porn terrorists and their client-agents who are waging a real war against our very real children. Our kids are the ones who are "virtual" targets of child-porn predators.

Thank God we have the First Amendment. It allows us to say directly that the damned-fool Supreme Court justices responsible for this abomination should be horsewhipped.[2]

---

2. In April 2003 Congress passed legislation that narrows the definition of pornography and creates new obscenity offenses to cover virtual and real child pornography that involves visual depictions of prepubescent children and minors. The law also creates a new offense against pandering visual depictions as child pornography and strengthens penalties for repeat offenders.

> "Virtual-porn prohibitions are especially
> easy to abuse."

Virtual Child Pornography Should Not Be Banned

Wendy Kaminer

According to Wendy Kaminer in the following viewpoint, virtual child pornography is protected speech because real children are not harmed in its production. The images depicted in virtual pornography are computer-generated, so real children are not forced to have sex, she argues. Moreover, Kaminer maintains that there is no evidence to suggest that virtual child pornography incites pedophiles to molest children. In April 2003 Congress passed legislation that tightened restrictions on real and virtual child pornography and strengthened penalties for repeat offenders. Kaminer is a senior correspondent for The American Prospect *and a contributing editor at* The Atlantic Monthly. *She also serves on the national board of the American Civil Liberties Union (ACLU).*

As you read, consider the following questions:

1. As reported by Wendy Kaminer, what does the Child Pornography Prevention Act (CPPA) of 1996 prohibit?

2. According to Kaminer, why do defenders of CPPA equate virtual with actual pornography?

3. Why does the ban on virtual child pornography depend on the subjective reaction of viewers?

It is possible, of course, that computer-simulated images of virtual children having virtual sex may encourage pedophiles to act on their impulses or may assist them in seducing children. There is, however, little or no empirical evidence that these images have such dire effects. Congress criminalized virtual child porn anyway.

The Child Pornography Prevention Act of 1996 (CPPA) prohibits computer images that "appear" to show actual children engaged in sex; it also bans advertising, promoting, or describing any sexually explicit images "in such a manner that conveys the impression" that actual children are depicted. Antiporn activists insist that this ban on virtual porn is essential to protecting children and enforcing laws against actual child pornography, since prosecutors may not be able to distinguish the actual from the virtual variety. Free-speech advocates charge that the CPPA allows for the prosecution of thought crimes, by criminalizing non-obscene renderings of imaginary children engaged in imaginary sex. The federal courts are divided on the constitutionality of this statute: It was struck down by the Ninth Circuit Court of Appeals and upheld by the First, Fourth, and 11th Circuit Courts. The issue is now before the Supreme Court.[1]

Many civil libertarians have long accepted (and supported) bans on depicting actual children engaged in actual sex. Traditional child-porn laws need not rely on speculation about the harm caused by the distribution of sexually explicit images involving minors; they can rely instead on the harm caused by the *production* of sexually explicit images involving minors.

1. In *Ashcroft v. Free Speech Coalition* in 2002, the Supreme Court decided that the First Amendment protects pornography or other sexual images that only appear to depict real children engaged in sex.

But laws against depictions of imaginary children can rely only on imaginary evidence of harm. As the Ninth Circuit . . . observed in *Free Speech Coalition v. Reno*: "Factual studies that establish the link between computer-generated child pornography and the subsequent sexual abuse of children apparently do not yet exist."[2] Indeed, in enacting the CPPA, Congress relied on the report of the pornography commission led by former Attorney General Edwin Meese in the 1980s, a study that addressed only the suspected harms of pornography involving actual children. In other words, the Ninth Circuit stressed, the CPPA relies on findings that "predate" the technology it targets.

Still, defenders of the CPPA equate actual and virtual porn, simply because they are difficult to distinguish visually. "Both actual and counterfeit child pornography will pass for the real thing and incite pedophiles to molest and children to be victims," according to a brief filed by the National Law Center for Children and Families and several other conservative advocacy groups. "If the pedophile and the child victim cannot tell the difference, there is no difference in the effect conveyed." What's wrong with this reasoning? (Put aside the callous disregard of the difference to real children who are forced to have sex in the production of real pornography.) It assumes its conclusion—that virtual child porn incites pedophilia and creates "child victims"—and it advocates criminalizing speech because of its presumed effect on a particular class of listeners: people inclined toward child abuse.

Courts confront this argument repeatedly in First Amendment cases, particularly in cases involving pornography. In 1985, in *American Booksellers Association v. Hudnut*, the Seventh Circuit Court of Appeals struck down a local antiporn ordinance that was based on the assumption that pornography leads to the objectification of women and contributes to

2. In 2001 the case was called *Free Speech Coalition v. Reno*; in 2002 the case became *Ashcroft v. Free Speech Coalition*.

An Indirect Link

Virtual child pornography is not "intrinsically related" to the sexual abuse of children. While the government asserts that the images can lead to actual instances of child abuse, the causal link is contingent and indirect. The harm does not necessarily follow from the speech, but depends upon some unquantified potential for subsequent criminal acts.

Anthony M. Kennedy,
Ashcroft v. Free Speech Coalition, *2002.*

sexual violence and discrimination. Accepting this assumption for the sake of argument, the appeals court pointed out its inadequacies: "All of these unhappy effects depend on mental intermediation." In others words, the power of speech is collaborative.

Since the ban on virtual child porn relies heavily on the subjective reactions of viewers, speakers are given little notice of precisely what speech is criminalized. When Congress bans sexually explicit material that "appears" to depict minors engaged in sex, you have to ask, "Appears to whom?" A lot of people over 40 have trouble distinguishing 19-year-olds from precocious 15-year-olds. The CPPA could easily be construed to prohibit non-obscene sexually explicit images of young adults. The statute does provide its targets with a defense: that the alleged child porn in fact involved an actual person, who was an adult at the time the image was produced (so this defense does not apply in cases of virtual child porn) and the image was not promoted in a way that "conveyed the impression" that it involved a minor. "Conveyed to whom?" you have to ask.

What are people talking about when they talk about child porn? That depends. Some point to Calvin Klein ads or the movie adaptations of *Lolita* (not to mention the book). *The Tin Drum*, a 1979 film based on a novel by Günter Grass, is considered pornographic in Oklahoma City: A few years ago, local officials confiscated copies of this allegedly dangerous film, which includes a scene suggestive of oral sex between a six-year-old boy and a teenage girl. A court in Oklahoma judged the film obscene.

Some supporters of CPPA will dismiss cases like this as "horror stories," suggesting that they're rare or even apocryphal. In fact, they're fairly common, as anyone familiar with the history of censorship knows. Virtual-porn prohibitions are especially easy to abuse, since evidence of social, scientific, or artistic value is irrelevant to a charge of child pornography. (Speech must be found to have no redeeming value to be considered obscene.) How will the CPPA be applied by a Justice Department led by right-wingers? Senator Jesse Helms includes some sex education materials in his definition of child porn.[3] Soon speech may be no safer than sex.

3. In April 2003 Congress passed legislation that narrows the definition of pornography and creates new obscenity offenses to cover virtual and real child pornography that involves visual depictions of prepubescent children and minors. The law also creates a new offense against pandering visual depictions as child pornography and strengthens penalties for repeat offenders.

For Further Discussion

Chapter 4

1. Francis Canavan argues that free expression is only valuable when it contributes to the good of society. The American Civil Liberties Union (ACLU) contends that free expression is always essential because it ensures the free exchange of ideas. With whose argument do you most agree? Citing from the texts, explain your answer.

2. According to Laura Leets, hate speech should be regulated because it may contribute to the rising incidence of hate crimes. Ted Gup maintains that hate speech should not be limited because open discussion of hateful ideas is critical to reducing bigotry in society. In your opinion, does hate speech contribute to violent crime? Or, do you think that hate speech performs a valuable function in society? Why or why not? Cite specific passages from the text(s) in your response.

3. Shawntel Smith asserts that desecrating the flag rejects the values that it represents: freedom, opportunity, and unity. Andrew Cohen argues that flags are personal property, and the values represented by the flag are not harmed by a person damaging his or her own property. Whose argument do you find most convincing and why? Cite specific passages from the text(s) in your response.

4. According to Paul M. Rodriguez, virtual child pornography should be banned because it may incite pedophiles to molest young children. Wendy Kaminer contends that virtual child pornography is computer-generated pictures of children engaged in sex acts, and no children were harmed in the making of it. Thus, she argues, virtual child pornography is protected free speech. Based

on the authors' arguments, do you think that virtual child pornography is a form of speech that should be protected? Why or why not? Cite specific passages from the text(s) in your response.

Periodical Bibliography

The following articles have been selected to supplement the diverse views presented in this chapter.

Anonymous. "The Assault on Civil Liberties: Speech and Assembly." *Progressive.* August 2000: 8. http://findarticles.com/p/articles/mi_m1295/is_8_64/ai_63904135/.

Blackford, Russell. "Free Speech and Hate Speech." *Quadrant.* 373 (January-February, 2001): 10–17.

Bork, Robert. "The Sanctity of Smut." *The Wall Street Journal.* April 27, 2002: A22. http://www.opinionjournal.com/extra/?id=105001991.

Goldberg, Jonah. "Free Speech Rots from the Inside Out." *American Enterprise for Public Policy Research.* 14.1 (January-February, 2003): 52.

Heins, Marjorie. "Screening Out Sex: Kids, Computers, and the New Censors." *American Prospect.* 39 (July 01, 1998): 38–44.

Hellinger, Daniel. "Taking Liberties with the Constitution." *Synthesis / Regeneration.* 28 (Spring 2002): 2–4, and http://www.greens.org/s-r/28/28-02.html.

Hentoff, Nat. "How Free Is Free Speech?" *World & I.* (April 2001).

Huff, James. "Filtering Behavior Instead of Speech." *American Libraries.* (April 1999): 38.

Kaminer, Wendy. "Bigots' Rights." *American Prospect.* June 19, 2000. http://www.prospect.org/cs/articles?article=bigots_rights.

———. "Virtual Offensiveness." *American Prospect.* November 19, 2001. http://www.prospect.org/cs/articles?article=virtual_offensiveness.

Kurtz, Stanley. "Free Speech and an Orthodoxy of Dissent." *Chronicle of Higher Education.* October 26, 2001. http://www.yale.edu/dsj/docs/Kurtz10-26-01.pdf.

Marshall, Joshua. "Will Free Speech Get Tangled in the Net?" *American Prospect.* January 01, 1998. http://www.prospect.org/cs/articles?article=will_free_speech_get_tangled_in_the_net.

Torralbas, Alex. "How the Net Endangers a Basic American Liberty." *Computerworld.* April 03, 2000. http://www.computerworld.com.au/article/105153/how_net_endangers_basic_american_liberty.

OPPOSING
VIEWPOINTS®
SERIES

CHAPTER 5

Addressing
Social Inequalities

Chapter Preface

In 1979 the Congressional Budget Office (CBO) began to collect data comparing income trends of Americans at different economic levels. The data collected since then suggests that the gap between the rich elite and the poor and middle classes is growing. In 1979 the average annual income (after taxes) of someone in the poorest 40 percentile was $18,695. Twenty-one years later, in 2000, that number had risen to $21,118. During that same time, however, the after-tax income of the wealthiest 1 percent of Americans more than tripled, from $286,300 to $862,700 (figures have been adjusted for inflation). In 1979 the total after-tax income of the wealthiest 1 percent of Americans was less than half of the total income of the bottom 40 percent; by 2000 the income of the wealthiest 1 percent had exceeded that of the poorest 40 percent of Americans.

Disagreements exist as to whether an increase in economic equality is a problem that must be solved by higher taxes on the wealthy or by other government actions. Some maintain that inequality is an inevitable and necessary component of America's free-market economy—a system they believe has made this nation a "land of opportunity" for those who work hard and have talent and good ideas. Economist Isabel V. Sawhill contends that "inequality reflects differences in individual talent and effort, and as such is a spur to higher economic growth, as well as just compensation for unequal effort and skill." She concludes that income inequality "is the price we pay for a dynamic economy." Like Sawhill, many Americans do not necessarily view income inequality as a problem. American attitudes toward inequality are shaped by the belief that those at the bottom can successfully work their way to the top—and that all Americans have a roughly equal opportunity to succeed on their own merits. "People accept inequality," asserts Purdue University sociologist Robert Perrucci, "if they think there is opportunity."

Others argue, however, that income inequality among families may create inequality of opportunity as well. Economist Michael D. Yates, in his book *Naming the System: Inequality and Work in the Global Economy*, asks readers to compare the lives of a child born to a high-income family in a fashionable neighborhood and another child raised by a single mom in an impoverished, crime-ridden ghetto. "Which mother will have the best health care? . . . Which child is more likely to get adequate nutrition and have good health care in early childhood? If the poor child does not have these things, who will return to this child the brain cells lost as a consequence? . . . Which child will go to the better school? Which will have access to books . . . and computers in the home?" Yates concludes that the United States must do more to equalize opportunities for its children.

As the Congressional Budget Office data suggest, the growing gap between the rich and poor is real. The debate now is what to do about the gap, if anything. The viewpoints in this chapter present various views on economic inequality in the United States and what social policies can best address it.

> "The ... persistent structural inequalities that continue to ... imprison African American experience are largely outside the parameters of polite public discussion."

African Americans Are Oppressed in American Society

Paul Street

Paul Street is a vice president at the Chicago Urban League, and his writings have appeared in Dissent, Monthly Review, *and other liberal and leftist publications. In the following viewpoint, he notes that Americans hold a widespread belief that racism is a thing of the past and that African Americans no longer face racial barriers. Street disagrees, however, arguing that while explicit and open racial bigotry may no longer be acceptable, black Americans are still victimized by a society that places them in the poorest neighborhoods and schools, leaves them with poorer medical care and economic opportunities, and singles them out for criminal prosecution and incarceration. Those who seek greater social justice in the United States must still confront America's continuing racial divide, he concludes.*

Paul Street, "Class, Color, and the Hidden Injuries of Race," Z Magazine, vol. 15, June 2002. Reproduced by permission of the author.

As you read, consider the following questions:

1. What is the missing element in the newspaper stories described by Paul Street to begin the viewpoint?

2. According to the author, what are African Americans being conditioned to think about their place in American society?

3. What are the responsibilities of liberals and leftists regarding race, according to Street?

Sometimes it's the silences that speak the loudest. Consider, for example, a study released last year [2001] by a team of public health researchers at the Children's Memorial Hospital in Chicago. As noted in a front-page *Chicago Sun-Times* story titled "Danger Zones for Kids," this study reported that injury was the leading cause of death for youth in the United States. The problem is especially great, its authors learned, in Chicago, where injuries killed 106 adolescents per year during the mid-1990s. Especially disturbing was the study's discovery that the city's youth mortality rate for "intentional injury," that is violence, was much higher than for accidental injury. The leading cause of "intentional injury" for Chicago kids over 10 years old was gun violence. Beyond citywide numbers, the researchers reported on the distribution of youth injuries and deaths across the city's 77 officially designated Community Areas. Neighborhood disparities, they found, were severe, ranging from one West Side community where 146 per 100,000 were hospitalized for injuries per year—more than 4 times the citywide average—to more than 30 neighborhoods where fewer than 6 youth were hospitalized for injuries.

Take a front-page *The New York Times* piece that appeared late last summer [2001] under the provocative title "Rural Towns Turn to Prisons to Re-ignite Their Economies." According to this article, rural America relies like never before on prison construction to produce jobs and economic development formerly provided by farms, factories, coal mines, and oil. Reporting that 25 new prisons went up in the United States countryside each year during the 1990s, up from 16 per year in the 1980s and just 4 per year in the 1970s, the article quoted an Oklahoma city manager to chilling effect. "There's no more recession-proof form of economic development," this official, whose town just got a shiny new maximum-security prison, told *The Times*, than incarceration because "nothing's going to stop crime."

A final example is provided by another front-page story in the *Chicago Tribune*. Last July [2001], the *Tribune* reported that Ford Heights, a desperately poor "inner-ring" suburb south of Chicago, led the nation in percentage of households headed by single mothers. This article included a map showing the United States' top 20 communities as ranked by percentage of single-mother households. While it related "Ford Heights' dubious title" to residents' poor education, weak job skills, and south-suburban de-industrialization, it especially emphasized residents' "self-defeating social patterns" including, naturally enough, teen sex. Echoing the findings of the latest academic poverty research, it noted a strong connection between teen pregnancy and young people's "hopeless" sense that the future holds little and there is little reason to "defer gratification."

Something Missing

Good, well-written reports and articles all. There was something curiously missing, however, from each. Strange though it may seem in one of the world's most racially segregated cities, the Children's Memorial team and the *Sun-Times* did not link their findings to readily available, recently released census data on the racial composition of Chicago's neighborhoods. They had to go out of their way not to make the connection. Of the city's top 20 Community Areas ranked by injury-related youth mortality, no less than 15 are currently 90 percent or more African American. All but one very disproportionately black for the city. By contrast, more than three-fourths of the 31 neighborhoods where just 6 or less injury-related youth hospitalizations occurred per year were very disproportionately white.

In a similar vein, the *Tribune* piece, while curiously including three photographs of African American Ford Heights teen moms, refrained from mentioning that all of the top 20 single-mom communities were very disproportionately African American. Seventy percent of those communities where youth feel especially hopeless are more than 90 percent black. All but one are at least two-thirds black. Nowhere, finally, could the liberal *Times* bring itself to mention the very predominantly white composition of the keepers and the very predominantly black composition of those kept in America's burgeoning new prison towns.

One has to go elsewhere than the nation's leading newspaper to learn that blacks are 12.3 percent of the U.S. population but comprise fully half of the roughly 2 million Americans currently behind bars. . . .

Color Blind

Under the rule of color-blind rhetoric, significant and widespread racism is largely a thing of the nation's past. There is a widespread belief among U.S. whites that African Americans now enjoy equal opportunity. "As white America sees it," write Leonard Steinhorn and Barbara Diggs-Brown in their sobering *By the Color of Our Skin: The Illusion of Integration and the Reality of Race* (2000), "every effort has been made to welcome blacks into the American mainstream, and now they're on their own. . . . 'We got the message, we made the corrections—get on with it.'"

In our current officially color-blind era of American history, older and more blatant forms and incidents of classic explicit and intentional racial bigotry are still fit subjects for open discussion. It helps if those forms and incidents are understood as anomalous and identified primarily with lower- and working-class whites who do not understand the new rules of the game. The more significant and persistent structural inequalities that continue to shape, limit, and imprison African American experience are largely outside the parameters of polite public discussion. The new reluctance to speak freely about race comes in conservative, liberal, and left forms. For conservatives, predictably, the conventional argument that racism is essentially over and that the main barrier to black advancement comes from within the black community, in the form of self-destructive behaviors and beliefs. There's nothing surprising in this reactionary racist sentiment, which parallels triumphant capitalist "end of history" wisdom on the related and supposed irrelevance of class and other barriers to freedom and democracy in the U.S.

There are now liberals who share the sense that racism has ceased to be a significant barrier to black well-being and success. Among liberals, and some further to the left, however, color-blind rhetoric appears more commonly in the argument that society will best serve blacks by downplaying the danger zone of race and emphasizing the shared dilemmas faced by all economically disadvantaged people regardless of color. . . .

Blame the Victim

Whatever form it takes, however, color-blind rhetoric and the "illusion of integration" it conveys render much of America's harshly divided social landscape shockingly unintelligible. The phenomena that are hopelessly muddled include an inequitably funded educational system that apparently just happens to provide poorer instruction for blacks than whites; an electoral system whose voting irregularities and domination by big money happens to disproportionately disenfranchise blacks; a criminal justice system that happens to especially stop, arrest, prosecute, and incarcerate African Americans; a political

White Privilege

Few whites have ever thought of our position as resulting from racial preferences. Indeed, we pride ourselves on our hard work and ambition, as if somehow we invented the concepts.

As if we have worked harder than the folks who were forced to pick cotton and build levies for free; harder than the Latino immigrants who spend 10 hours a day in fields picking strawberries or tomatoes; harder than the (mostly) women of color who clean hotel rooms or change bedpans in hospitals, or the (mostly) men of color who collect our garbage.

We strike the pose of self-sufficiency while ignoring the advantages we have been afforded in every realm of activity: housing, education, employment, criminal justice, politics, banking and business. We ignore the fact that at almost every turn, our hard work has been met with access to an opportunity structure denied to millions of others. Privilege, to us, is like water to the fish: invisible precisely because we cannot imagine life without it.

Tim Wise, AlterNet, *February 20, 2003.*

economy whose tendency toward sharp inequality happens to especially impoverish and divide black communities; and residential markets and housing practices that happen to disproportionately restrict African American children to the poorest and most dangerous neighborhoods and communities, where kids' chances of learning are significantly diminished by the threats of injury and violence. The list goes on.

Worse, Americans trained to believe that all the relevant racial barriers have been torn down are conditioned to think that the nation's millions of truly disadvantaged African Americans have no one but themselves to blame for their persistent pain and disproportionate presence at the bottom of the American hierarchy. That thought lies at the heart of America's new color-blind racism, which draws ironic strength from the relative decline of acceptable explicit racial bigotry in American life. It is at the core of the hesitancy some liberals and progressives feel about speaking openly on race. It makes well-intentioned anti-racist liberals and leftists reluctant to fully examine the color of modern social problems, for to do so in the current ideological context is, they reason, with some justice, to fuel the fires of new racist (color-blind) victim-blaming and even to damage black self-esteem. . . .

But liberals and leftists will not create the color-blind society of which Martin Luther King Jr. so famously dreamed by acting as if it has already arrived. Intellectuals and activists will not answer mainstream denial of racism's deep and stubborn persistence nor respond effectively to the attack on structural understandings of racial inequality by relegating race to the forgotten footnotes. They will carry the moral and political responsibility to write and speak about race and racism as long as skin color continues to significantly shape dominant social, political, and economic structures of opportunity and outcome. To discuss racial differences without reference to cross-racial questions of economic inequality and political economy is to further the racial divide in a way that thwarts social justice and democracy in general.

▌ "Nobody *is oppressed in America.*"

African Americans Are Not Oppressed in American Society

David Horowitz

Author and civil rights activist David Horowitz is the president of the Center for the Study of Popular Culture. His books include Hating Whitey: And Other Progressive Causes *and* The Politics of Bad Faith. *In the following viewpoint, he argues that American society does not oppress African Americans or other minority groups. Rather, he contends, political leftists have a stake in pretending that such racial oppression exists. The pathologies found within black communities, such as high crime and incarceration rates and poor education, cannot be blamed on institutional racism, he argues.*

As you read, consider the following questions:

1. Why are people afraid to speak out about the problems of African Americans, according to David Horowitz?

2. What is the difference between oppression and bigotry, according to the author?

David Horowitz, "Nobody Is Oppressed in America," *Ex femina*, January 2000. Reproduced with permission by Independent Women's Forum, www.iwf.org.

3. What does the story of Oprah Winfrey say about American society, according to Horowitz?

My book [*Hating Whitey: And Other Progressive Causes*] is about race and the double standard that exists in American life. We live in a country where part of the social contract is that it is wrong and unacceptable to be intolerant or to hate another ethnic group. Yet there is a license to hate white people in our culture, and, in fact, the hatred of whites is positively incited at our elite universities.

I got into trouble with these ideas when I wrote a piece for the Internet magazine *Salon*. As a result of that article, Jack White said that I was a racist in his column in *TIME* magazine. *TIME* actually ran the headline "A Real Live Bigot." It is not pleasant to be called a racist by *TIME* magazine, but that is why there is silence on this issue. People are afraid to speak out because they don't want to be called racists. My book is an attempt to speak out, an attempt to provoke a new level of dialog.

A Crippling Message

We have come to a point where if there are too many blacks in jail, the obvious problem—that too many blacks are committing crimes—is not even addressed. It's white racism that accounts for the excessive numbers of blacks in jail. If black kids are not passing tests and are not up to grade level, instead of looking to their parents and their community for a lack of support, or to the schools that are crumbling, we hear that the cause is institutional racism. "Blame whitey" is the idea. Every pathology in the inner-city black communities is blamed on white people.

So, the first thing you can see about this is the crippling message that is being sent to the black community. You have no power to affect your own destiny since white people control everything.

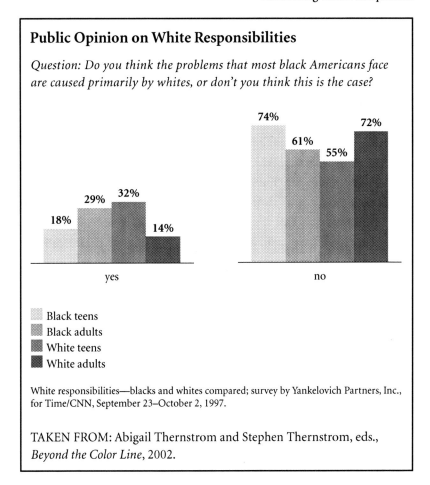

Public Opinion on White Responsibilities

Question: Do you think the problems that most black Americans face are caused primarily by whites, or don't you think this is the case?

Black teens
Black adults
White teens
White adults

White responsibilities—blacks and whites compared; survey by Yankelovich Partners, Inc., for Time/CNN, September 23–October 2, 1997.

TAKEN FROM: Abigail Thernstrom and Stephen Thernstrom, eds., *Beyond the Color Line*, 2002.

The Left has a vested interest in there being oppressors and oppressed people, and one of the things that really upset Jack White was my statement—which I frequently make when I'm on campuses—that *nobody* is oppressed in America, except maybe children by their abusive parents.

Oppression is a group phenomenon, and there's no way out if you're oppressed. It's different from bigotry, which is an individual matter.

There are millions of refugees from oppressive regimes; that's why we can call them oppressive. They leave their country if they have the freedom to leave. But there's nobody leaving America. There's no exodus from America by black people or brown people. Quite the contrary. They all want to come here. If America is a racist, oppressive country, how come the Haitians want to come here? Why do they want to risk their lives to get to America? To be oppressed? No, once you get the ideological blinders off, and you just think about it for two seconds, you know why they come: They have more rights and more opportunities in America as black Haitians than they do in black-run Haiti. . . .

I was speaking at Bates College and a young woman asked me, "What about the hierarchies?" Perhaps you're not aware that your children are being taught in every university in America that there are hierarchies of race, class, and gender that oppress designated oppressed groups? So, I said to this young woman, where do you put Oprah Winfrey in your hierarchies? She was the daughter of a Mississippi sharecropper, and she was abused as a child. There was no affirmative action committee telling the television industry that we needed, for diversity purposes, a black female to do a talk show. She clawed her way up, and by her intelligence and her ability, she basically drove Phil Donahue out of the business.

So you can just compact the zillion words of text of all the women's studies courses in America and all of the African American studies and put them to some better use, because the entire edifice of leftist theory on race and gender is completely demolished by the example of Oprah Winfrey. It's very hard to make a leftist see it, but that is the reality.

"Affirmative action was . . . [a] way of trying to redress the wrongs of the past and prepare the nation for a future of equality."

Affirmative Action Programs Promote Justice for African Americans

E.A. Rohrbach-Perry

E.A. Rohrbach-Perry is a United Methodist minister in Pennsylvania. In the following viewpoint, she argues that affirmative action programs for African Americans are necessary, both to redress past wrongs against African Americans and to counter ongoing discrimination against them. Because many African Americans are still being denied jobs and economic opportunity because of their race, she contends, such programs remain a necessary step toward creating a truly just and equal society.

As you read, consider the following questions:

1. What families does E.A. Rohrbach-Perry use as examples of continuing racial discrimination in the United States?

2. What percentage of the American public supports affirmative action, according to the author?

E.A. Rohrbach-Perry, "Color Still Holds People Back," *Progressive Populist*, May 15, 2004. © 2004 by E.A. Rohrbach-Perry. Reproduced by permission.

3. Why will affirmative action continue to be a hotly debated topic for some time to come, according to Rohrbach-Perry?

M arge is 38 and has four children, the oldest is in the Air Force. Over the years, she's had a variety of jobs, everything from babysitting to janitorial work. The job she liked best was that of a housekeeper at an upscale hotel in her hometown. Permanently laid off after Sept. 11, 2001, she misses that job. "I liked the work. It's easy; I was comfortable with it. I have four kids; I'm used to housekeeping!"

Interviewed in the food pantry waiting room, Marge explained how hard she worked to get that job. She filled out seven applications but was never contacted. Finally, a friend employed by the hotel called her, saying, "Someone didn't show up for work today—I told them you were a hard worker! Get in here fast!" Marge caught a bus to the hotel, filled out her eighth application, and began work that very day.

She thinks it's typical of the area she lives in—if you are a person of color you have to know someone to get a job.

Racial Discrimination

Shirley believes the same thing. She and her husband are an interracial couple and her husband has been having trouble finding work. When they lived in a shoreline resort community, the situation was different she said. The community had an international feel with great diversity of people and her African American husband was busily employed remodeling homes.

They moved to the northeast because of her mother's declining health and he hasn't been able to find steady employment since then. During good weather, he's been able to get some landscaping work but, during the winter, she brags, "He's a good househusband!"

It's the stereotypes that are holding them back, Shirley thinks. What kind of a place is it where a hard-working person can't get a job because the employer makes decisions based on racial stereotypes?

Fifty-four percent of Americans, according to a CBS News/ *The New York Times* poll, agree that America shouldn't be that kind of place. They support affirmative action programs in employment and educational settings—up 13% from just five years ago [1998]. Only 37% percent of Americans oppose affirmative action—and that number is down 10% from 1998.

Unfortunately, in that 37% reside some very influential people—the president of the United States, for example. George W. Bush, on Jan. 16 [2003], announced that his administration would support the Supreme Court challenge to the University of Michigan's affirmative action admissions policy. The university uses a point system for admissions and being African American earns applicants a specific number of points. Three Euro American applicants have filed the case against the university, saying they were denied admissions because the system gives preferences based on race. The president agrees, claiming that the university's system is unconstitutional.[1]

Affirmative Action

The heart of affirmative action lies in the 1965 actions of another president, Lyndon B. Johnson. He introduced the program as a way of addressing discrimination that lingered long after civil rights laws were passed. Of a four-century history in the United States, African Americans spent almost 250 years in slavery and another hundred years in legalized discrimination. Affirmative action was Johnson's way of trying to redress

1. In June 2003 the Supreme Court ruled that the point system used by the University of Michigan for undergraduate admissions was unconstitutional. But it also upheld a University of Michigan Law School admissions policy that favored minorities, affirming that race can be used in university admission decisions.

Affirmative Action and Justice

America has had over 200 years to deliver true justice, freedom, and equality to women and people of color. To believe that it now will make good the promise of equality without some kind of legislation to assist it is to engage in fantasy.

In advocating for affirmative action policies, people of color are not looking for government handouts. They merely are asking that some mechanism be kept in place to help provide the same social and economic opportunities most whites have had and continue to have access to.

Wilbert Jenkins, USA Today, *September 1999.*

the wrongs of the past and prepare the nation for a future of equality where the American Dream would be available to everyone.

In the four decades since Johnson's time, affirmative action has increased opportunities for many people to realize that dream through education and employment. While legalized discrimination died decades ago, racism still lives on. We can see it in the growth of Klan groups, Neo-Nazi groups and hate crimes. (See www.splcenter.org/intelligenceproject/ip-index.html.) The affirmative action programs have stood as a continuing attempt to defeat discrimination among those who have not yet understood that racism is not a part of the American Dream.

In that time, affirmative action has also raised criticism that opportunities given to African Americans were being taken away from Euro Americans. Emotive terms like "reverse discrimination," "quotas," and "preferences" were aimed at affirmative action, and the program was accused of giving preferential treatment to people with lower qualifications simply because of their race. Attempts have been made to dismantle the program and the University of Michigan case will most likely be an arena for heightened reactionary rhetoric.

However, the 54% majority of Americans won't be silent, either. "Angry White Guys for Affirmative Action" marched on Washington on April 1 [2003]—the date the Supreme Court heard the case—to support the University of Michigan's admissions policy. They claim the first affirmative action program was actually the college draft deferment that many Euro American men received during the Vietnam conflict—and that federal programs supporting home ownership are also affirmative action programs that primarily benefit Euro Americans. . . .

The Debate Continues

Whatever decision the Supreme Court makes, disagreements about affirmative action will probably continue. Those who believe in Johnson's hope of equality in education and employment will continue to support the program. Those who fear that they will lose something of their own with the expansion of opportunities for others will continue to denounce it and work for its dismantling. The president's participation in the Supreme Court case will make sure that affirmative action is a political topic of discussion for some time to come.

Meanwhile, as the words fly, people like Marge and her four children, Shirley and her husband, will try to get jobs. Once a month, they will pick up three days' worth of food at the food pantry. And they will continue to believe that if it wasn't for the color of their skin, they would have a job, earn a living, and be building the American Dream.

> *"Affirmative action uses unjust methods to address the wrong problems, and this is why it encounters resentment."*

Affirmative Action Programs Are Unjust

Steven Yates

In the following viewpoint, Steven Yates argues that affirmative action programs are an example of how a collectivist conception of social justice harms individuals. White Americans are having their chances at college admissions and employment lowered by affirmative action programs favoring African Americans, even though they bear no individual responsibility for slavery and discrimination against minorities, he maintains. Yates, an adjunct scholar with the Ludwig von Mises Institute and founder of the Worldviews Project, has a PhD in philosophy and has taught the subject full time for seven years. His published writings include academic articles and reviews and the book Civil Wrongs: What Went Wrong with Affirmative Action *(1994).*

Steven Yates, "Affirmative Action: Another Side to the Story," in LewRockwell.com, January 12, 2004. Reproduced by permission of the publisher and author. Steven Yates has a Ph.D. in philosophy and is the author of *Civil Wrongs: What Went Wrong With Affirmative Action* (San Francisco: ICS Press, 1994) as well as numerous articles in both refereed journals and online. He currently teaches philosophy at the University of South Carolina Upstate in Spartanburg, South Carolina.

As you read, consider the following questions:

1. What analogy does Steven Yates use to criticize affirmative action?

2. How does the author define *individualism* and *collectivism*?

3. What trends in American society does Yates criticize?

If a white man expresses objections to affirmative action programs, must his motives be racist?. . .

I have written this [viewpoint] for two reasons. One is to express this other side of the affirmative action story. Let's try an analogy.

A Basketball Analogy

Consider a basketball season in which certain teams play by all the familiar rules and others are compelled to play with each player having one arm tied behind his back.

No one, of course, would consider such games fair.

Now suppose someone proposed that for the next several seasons those teams whose players had been untied, were now to play all their games with an arm tied behind their backs, while those who had been tied up, now had both arms free.

Would turnabout be fair play?

Before answering, let's improve the analogy. Let's observe that there has been a complete turnover of players. All those who played in the first set of games have retired. The current players, therefore, are newcomers none of whom were involved with the original practice.

Now let's ask again: Would turnabout be fair?

To answer *yes* is to embrace affirmative action. To answer *no* is to reject it, on the grounds that the original perpetrators and beneficiaries of discrimination against blacks are gone (as are their victims), while those forced to sacrifice job opportunities, college admissions, etc., were unborn and so hardly responsible for the wrongs.

Individualism vs. Collectivism

My analogy contains a crucial premise, and it is important to identify it. It focuses on the players as individuals, not as members of collectives. Is it fair or just to penalize the children of a given race for wrongs perpetrated by their remote ancestors?

To say *no* is to take up for an *individualist* model of society, as opposed to a *collectivist* one. The former takes the individual as the most basic unit for analysis; the latter, the group.

Most of human history has been dominated by various sorts of collectivism. It is the easy point of view, the one that divides the human race into tribes. Its logic: you are either part of the tribe or an outcast—probably an enemy. This is why so much of our history is a history of wars and bloodshed.

Individualism began its slow rise only in the West, through the gradual convergence of Protestant Christianity, natural-rights political philosophy, and constitutional-republicanism, which saw a written Constitution as encoding the rights of individuals (not groups) that pre-exist government. Individualism is the hard point of view. Escaping tribalism took centuries.

Americans have never been fully consistent individualists. Otherwise the Framers would have gotten rid of slavery at the country's founding. Their not doing so was a blunder of major proportions.

Individualism is nevertheless the superior account of the human condition. There is no collective brain or nervous system. Individuals, not groups, take actions. To the extent that rights are acknowledged as belonging to individuals, societies have prospered. To the extent that human beings have been categorized as groups and moved about by force, societies have stagnated or declined. Marxism, the 20th century's domi-

A Moral Failure

Preferences must ... be judged a moral failure. Although some individuals have benefited significantly from preferences and a case can be made that preferences have enhanced the economic position of the black middle class, these gains have come at a great moral cost. Put simply, preferences discriminate. They deny opportunities to individuals solely because they are members of a nonpreferred race, gender, or ethnic group. The ambitions and aspirations, the hopes and dreams of individual Americans for themselves and for their families are trampled underfoot not for any wrongs those individuals have committed but for the sake of a bureaucratic effort to counterbalance the supposedly pervasive racism of American society. The penalty for the sins of the society at large is imposed on individuals who themselves are guilty only of being born a member of a nonpreferred group. Individual American citizens who would otherwise enjoy jobs and other opportunities are told that they must be denied in order to tilt the scales of racial justice.

Although preferences are presented as a remedial measure, they in fact create a class of innocent victims of government-imposed discrimination.

Charles T. Canady, Policy Review, *January/February 1998.*

nant form of collectivism, enslaved and impoverished a third of the human race. The final truth of collectivism is that it doesn't work. Period.

Who Is Responsible for Discrimination?

It therefore behooves us to look at such things as institutional, systemic discrimination to see who is responsible. We see not a collective entity, the "white race," but specific acts of government. These include Supreme Court decisions such as *Plessy v. Ferguson* and also legislation such as 1931's Davis-Bacon Act that made systemic discrimination convenient (it protected unionized workers, and most blacks were not unionized). It also behooves us to look for proximate causes of black disadvantage. Here one sees teen pregnancies, single-parent homes, broken families, substance abuse, and the violent nihilism of the "gangsta rap" culture. Men and women of good conscience—of whatever ethnicity—who would see the plight of black citizens of this country improve must address these real issues, not appeal to that bogey of political correctness, the "legacy of slavery," an institution that hasn't existed for almost 140 years. Once we have done this, I believe we will find that affirmative action uses unjust methods to address the wrong problems, and this is why it encounters resentment and passive resistance.

I mentioned two reasons for writing this [viewpoint]. Everything up till now was the first. The second: I am curious to see whether an ordinary white guy who knows good and well he hasn't reaped some mysterious benefit from being born white can write an article like this and not be demonized (by associates, other commentators, readers) as a covert racist. I have held out for individualism. But with the meteoric rise of political correctness, the complacent acceptance of unlimited immigration, and the dominance of academic ideologies of "diversity" and the "politics of identity," we are now moving backwards towards a society more and more divided into mutually distrustful collectives.

"A debt is owed, and it must be paid in full."

Slavery Reparations Would Promote Social Justice

Manning Marable

More than 135 years after slavery ended in the United States, people are debating whether the descendants of slaves should be compensated for their ancestors' suffering and unpaid labor. In the following viewpoint, Manning Marable maintains that African Americans deserve such reparations from the federal government and corporations who profited from slavery. He argues that while white Americans alive today are not guilty of enslaving anyone, they continue to benefit from slavery's legacy. He further argues that white Americans bear a collective responsibility for slavery and the continuing mistreatment of African Americans. Marable is a professor of African American studies at Columbia University and the author of numerous books on race and class in the United States, including Beyond Black and White: Race in America's Past, Present, and Future *and* How Capitalism Underdeveloped Black America.

Manning Marable, "In Defense of Black Reparations," ZNET (Zmag.org), October 30, 2002. Reproduced by permission of the author.

As you read, consider the following questions:

1. What does the American public believe about slavery reparations, according to Manning Marable?

2. What are some of the conservative arguments against reparations that the author attempts to rebut?

3. What is the greatest challenge facing the reparations movement, according to Marable?

Throughout this year [2002], the black reparations debate has become widely known, and it continued to attract increased national and international attention. In February 2002, CNN and *USA Today* commissioned the Gallup organization to conduct a national poll to assess public opinion on the issue. The results seemed to directly mirror the nation's parallel racial universes that are reproduced by structural racism.

When asked whether "corporations that made profits from slavery should apologize to black Americans who are descendants of slaves," 68 percent of African Americans responded affirmatively, with 23 percent opposed, while 62 percent of all whites rejected the call for an apology, with only 34 percent supporting it.

On the question of financial compensation, however, whites closed ranks around their racial privileges. When asked whether corporations benefiting from slave exploitation should "make cash payments to black Americans who are the descendants of slaves," 84 percent of all whites responded negatively, with only 11 percent supporting payments. A clear majority of African Americans polled, by contrast, endorsed corporate restitution payments, by a 57 to 35 percent margin, with 8 percent expressing no opinion.

When asked if the government should grant "cash payments" to blacks, nine out of ten white Americans rejected the proposal, while a strong majority of blacks favored it, by 55 to 37 percent. . . .

Answering Arguments

It was inevitable that as the demand for reparations achieved majority support among African Americans, black conservatives would be trotted out to defend the preservation of white power and privilege. The premier black apologist for the worst policies of the [President Ronald] Reagan administration in the black community, economist Thomas Sowell, declared that "the first thing to understand about the issue of reparations is that no money is going to be paid."

Sowell argued that the reparations cause was nothing more than an elaborate plot by black "demagogues," because "they are demanding something they know they are not going to get. But if we start operating on the principle that people alive today are responsible for what their ancestors did in centuries past, we will be adopting a principle that can tear any society apart, especially a multiethnic society like the United States."

Conservative economist Walter Williams seconded Sowell's objections, observing that "the problem, of course, is both slaves as well as their owners are all dead. What moral principle justifies forcing a white of today to pay a black of today for what a white of yesteryear did to a black of yesteryear?". . .

Younger black neoconservatives such as John McWhorter pointed out that even if the reparations movement succeeded in its efforts to create a national "slavery fund" to provide new resources to impoverished black communities, it would only reproduce the unequal structures of black dependency. "The reparation crowd's move from individual checks to a general fund will allow community-wide assistance," McWhorter admitted, "but this model has done nothing for forty years now. Who would get the money? For what purpose?"

The black conservatives' criticisms and complaints can easily be addressed. First, there is a crucial difference between "guilt" and "responsibility." White Americans who are alive today are not guilty of enslaving anyone, in the legal definition of the term. Most white Americans below the age of fifty played no role in directly supporting Jim Crow segregation and are not guilty of overt acts to block the integration of public accommodations and schools.

But white Americans, as a group, continue to be the direct beneficiaries of the legal apparatuses of white supremacy, carried out by the full weight of America's legal, political, and economic institutions. The consequences of state-sponsored racial inequality created a mountain of historically constructed, accumulated disadvantage for African Americans as a group.

Racism's Living Legacy

The living legacy of that racialized, accumulated disadvantage can easily be measured by looking at the gross racial deficits that segment Americans by race, in their life expectancies and in their unequal access to home ownership, business development, and quality education. The U.S. government, for nearly two centuries, established the legal parameters for corporations to carry out blatantly discriminatory policies and practices.

Consequently, it is insufficient for us to simply say that once the Jim Crow laws were changed, the state's responsibility to redress those victimized by discriminatory public policies ended. The U.S. government and the various state governments that created and perpetuated legal racial disparities are "responsible" for compensating the victims and their descendants. As citizens of this country, whites must bear the financial burden of the crimes against humanity that were carried out by their own government.

Another way of thinking about this is to point to the fiscal mismanagement and repressive social policies of the Reagan administration two decades ago. Billions of dollars of tax money paid by blacks and whites alike were allocated to the military industrial complex to finance global military inter-

Reparations and Social Justice

If we think of reparations as part of a broad strategy to radically transform society—redistributing wealth, creating a democratic and caring public culture, exposing the ways capitalism and slavery produced massive inequality—then the ongoing struggle for reparations holds enormous promise for revitalizing movements for social justice. . . .

The argument for reparations . . . shows how more than two centuries of U.S. policy facilitated accumulation among white property owners while further impoverishing African Americans. Thus federal assistance to black people in any form is not a gift but a down payment for centuries of unpaid labor, violence, and exploitation.

Robin D.G. Kelley,
Against the Current, *January/February 2003.*

ventions and a nuclear arms race. The vast majority of African Americans strongly opposed these reactionary policies.

We were not "guilty" of participating in the decisions to carry out such policies. Yet, as citizens, we are "responsible" for paying to finance Reagan's disastrous militarism, which left the country deeply in debt. We have an obligation under law to pay taxes. Thus, all citizens of the United States have the same "responsibility" to compensate members of their own society that were deliberately stigmatized by legal racism. Individual "guilt" or "innocence" is therefore irrelevant.

America's version of legal apartheid created the conditions of white privilege and black subordination that we see all around us every day. A debt is owed, and it must be paid in full. . . .

What reparations does is to force whites to acknowledge the brutal reality of our common history, something white society generally has refused to do. It provides a historically grounded explanation for the continuing burden of racial oppression: the unequal distribution of economic resources, land, and access to opportunities for social development, which was sanctioned by the federal government.

Consequently it is that same government that bears the responsibility of compensating those citizens and their descendants to whom constitutional rights were denied. Affirmative action was essentially "paycheck equality," in the words of political scientist Ronald Waiters; it created millions of job opportunities, but did relatively little to transfer wealth from one racial group to another.

One-third of all African American households today have a negative net wealth. The average black household's wealth is less than 15 percent of the typical white household's. Most of our people are trapped in an almost bottomless economic pit from which there will be no escape—unless we change our political demands and strategy from liberal integrationism to a restructuring of economic resources, and the elimination of structural deficits that separate blacks and whites into unequal racial universes.

From Handout to Payback

"Reparations" transforms the dynamics of the national racial discourse, moving from "handouts" to "paybacks." It parallels a global movement by people of African descent and other third world people to renegotiate debt and to demand compensation for slavery, colonialism, and apartheid. . . .

"Economic reparations" could take a variety of forms, any of which could be practically implemented. I favor the establishment of a reparations social fund that would channel federal, state, and/or corporate funds for investment in nonprofit,

Lasting Repercussions

In response to our call [for black reparations], individual Americans need not feel defensive or under attack. No one holds any living person responsible for slavery or the later century-plus of legal relegation of blacks to substandard education, exclusion from home ownership via restrictive covenants and redlining, or any of the myriad of mechanisms for pushing blacks to the back of the line. Nonetheless, we must all, as a nation, ponder the repercussions of those acts.

Randall Robinson,
Nation, *March 13, 2000.*

community-based organizations, economic empowerment zones in areas with high rates of unemployment, and grants or interest-free loans for blacks to purchase homes or to start businesses in economically depressed neighborhoods.

However, there are other approaches to the reconstruction of black economic opportunity. Sociologist Dalton Conley has suggested the processing of "individual checks via the tax system, like a refundable slavery tax credit." Major corporations and banks that were "unjustly enriched" by either slave labor or by Jim Crow-era discriminatory policies against African Americans could set aside a portion of future profits in a trust fund to financially compensate their victims and their descendants.

Universities whose endowments were based on the slave trade or on slave labor and/or companies that were unjustly enriched by racial segregation laws could create scholarship funds to give greater access to African American students.

Challenges to the Reparations Movement

It would be dangerous and foolish for the proponents of reparations to quarrel among themselves over the best approach for implementation at this time. Over a generation ago, there were numerous divisions within the civil rights movement, separating leaders and rival organizations. They all agreed on the general goal, the abolition of legal racial segregation, but espoused very different ways and tactics to get there. The same model should be applied to reparations.

Any effort to impose rigid ideological or organizational conformity on this diverse and growing popular movement will only serve to disrupt and destroy it.

As I have written previously, the greatest challenge in the national debate over African American reparations is in convincing black people, not whites, that we can actually win. The greatest struggle of the oppressed is always against their own weaknesses, doubts, and fears. The reparations demand is most liberating because it has the potential for transforming how black people see themselves, and our own history.

> *"Paying the descendants of slaves a monetary settlement today, more than 135 years after slavery ended, will do nothing."*

Slavery Reparations Would Not Promote Social Justice

Linda Chavez

Linda Chavez is a columnist and the president of the Center for Equal Opportunity. Her writings include An Unlikely Conservative: The Transformation of an Ex-Liberal (or How I Became the Most Hated Hispanic in America). *In the viewpoint that follows, she concedes that slavery was an unjust chapter in American history and that slaves should have been compensated immediately after slavery was abolished. But she goes on to assert that financial reparations for the descendants of American slaves are not the way to redress slavery or attain justice for African Americans. It is impossible to determine who should make or receive such payments more than a century after slavery's demise, Chavez maintains.*

Linda Chavez, "America's Original Sin," townhall.com, May 30, 2001. By permission of Linda Chavez and Creators Syndicate, Inc.

As you read, consider the following questions:

1. What is the real impetus behind the movement for reparations, according to Linda Chavez?

2. How have black Americans been unjustly treated in the past, according to the author?

3. What alternative to "writing a check" does Chavez propose for redressing the past injustices of slavery?

If it were possible to wipe out the legacy of slavery by writing a big, fat check, I'd be all for it. Who wouldn't be in favor of a simple solution to the problems that plague much of the African American community in America today—especially since all of us are affected, not just blacks? Imagine, a one-time payment that would solve family breakdown, poverty and homicide among young, black males. But there are no easy solutions, and the payment of reparations to the descendants of slaves certainly isn't the answer. It's just more of the same liberal cure-all: Let government redistribute money from one group to try to solve the problems of another.

The reparations movement got a big boost this week [May 30, 2001] when one of America's most distinguished newspapers, *The Philadelphia Inquirer*, endorsed the concept in an editorial. But the real impetus behind the reparations campaign is the grievance industry—that group of professional guilt-mongers who hope to enrich themselves by claiming to represent the downtrodden.

An Indelible Stain

There is no question that slavery indelibly stains American history. How is it that a nation founded on the principle that all men are created equal could perpetuate a system in which some men owned others, like mere chattel? But 140,000 Union soldiers died to expiate slavery, so to suggest that no white Americans ever suffered for the sins of slavery is simply wrong.

By permission Asay and Creators Syndicate, Inc.

Still, slaves should have been compensated immediately after the Civil War for the great harm they endured. Congress promised, then failed to deliver, 40 acres and a mule to every former slave. The course of American history might well have been different had all the reforms promised to the Freedmen's Bureau been enacted. As it was, of the post-Civil War amendments passed by Congress to right the wrongs of American slavery, only the 13th Amendment, which abolished slavery, was fully implemented. The 14th Amendment, which guaranteed equal protection of the laws, and the 15th Amendment, which guaranteed blacks the right to vote, were universally ignored in the Deep South and throughout much of the nation for more than 100 years after they were adopted.

The failure to do what was right at the time has cost this country greatly. As Gunnar Myrdal wrote more than 50 years ago in his great treatise on America's race problems, *An American Dilemma*, virtually all of the social problems encountered in the black community can be traced back to slavery and the era of Jim Crow laws, which deprived blacks of their most basic rights. But the question is, how do you solve those problems now?

Payment Raises Questions

Paying the descendants of slaves a monetary settlement today, more than 135 years after slavery ended, will do nothing. Nor is it possible to determine who should receive payments and who should pay them. Some African Americans are descended from persons who came to the United States long after slavery was abolished, including the thousands of Haitians, Dominicans and other Caribbean immigrants of the last 30 years. These persons' ancestors may have been slaves in their native land, but should the United States have to pay for the sins of all slave-owning nations?

More importantly, why should Americans whose ancestors did not benefit from slavery, or who may not even have lived in the United States at the time slavery existed, have to pay for these sins? Indeed it is a new variation on punishing the sons for the sins of the fathers to insist that all whites who live in the United States today must compensate all blacks who happen to live here now. Most whites are not descended from slave-owners. Nor are they the beneficiaries of ill-begotten gains from slavery, which hampered—not helped—the early American economy. The South remained an economic backwater from the 19th century until the modern civil rights era, in large part because the region failed to take advantage of its best resource: human capital. Discrimination on the basis of race is bad business, and the South failed to thrive until it put aside officially sanctioned racism.

Slavery will always remain America's Original Sin. But the best way to absolve ourselves is not by writing a check but by resolving never again to treat another human being as less than our equal because of the color of his skin.

For Further Discussion

Chapter 5

1. Paul Street argues that many social phenomena in America make sense if viewed through the prism of race. In which of his examples do you find the connection to racism to be the strongest? The weakest? Cite specific passages from the text(s) in your response.

2. In your opinion, does the example of one person—Oprah Winfrey—constitute a decisive argument against racial oppression in America, as David Horowitz suggests? Why or why not? Cite specific passages from the text(s) in your response.

3. E.A. Rohrbach-Perry cites the story of one family as an example of why affirmative action is necessary. Is her use of a single example more or less persuasive than Horowitz's example of Oprah Winfrey? Defend your answer using specific passages from the text in your response.

4. What do you make of Steven Yates's basketball analogy in his attack on affirmative action programs: Does his analogy accurately depict what affirmative action entails, in your opinion? Why or why not? Cite specific passages from the text in your response.

5. Steven Yates identifies himself as a white man in his attack on affirmative action. What point do you believe he is attempting to make by such an identification? Do you believe that his race is relevant in critiquing his arguments? Are attacks on affirmative action more credible in your mind if they come from a member of a minority group? Why or why not? Cite specific passages from the text(s) in your response.

6. Linda Chavez concedes that slavery is an evil and that slaves should have been compensated after the Civil War. Why does she then oppose slavery reparations today? After reading the arguments of Chavez and Manning Marable, do you believe that African Americans should, as a matter of justice, receive financial compensation? Explain your answer citing specific passages from the text in your response.

Periodical Bibliography

The following articles have been selected to supplement the diverse views presented in this chapter.

Bérubé, Michael. "And Justice for All." *Nation*. (January 24, 2005): 27. http://www.thenation.com/doc/20050124/berube.

Chappell, David L. "If Affirmative Action Fails . . . What Then?" *The New York Times*. (May 8, 2004): B7. http://www.nytimes.com/2004/05/08/books/an-essay-if-affirmative-action-fails-what-then.html?pagewanted=1.

Dias, Maria Clara. "Affirmative Action and Social Justice." *Connecticut Law Review*. 36.3 (Spring 2004): 871–878.

Edmundson, Mark. "Civil Disobedience Against Affirmative Action." *The New York Times Magazine*. (December 14, 2003): 60.

Hoar, William P. "Benign Discrimination?" *New American*. 19.9 (May 5, 2003): 42–44.

Leo, John. "Enslaved to the Past." *U.S. News & World Report*. (April 15, 2002): 39.

Marable, Manning. "An Idea Whose Time Has Come . . . Whites Have an Obligation to Recognize Slavery's Legacy." *Newsweek*. (August 27, 2001): 22, and http://www.hartford-hwp.com/archives/45/323.html.

Matthews, Chris. "White Blindness." *San Francisco Chronicle*. (July 15, 2001): C4, and http://www.sfgate.com/cgi-bin/article.cgi?f=/c/a/2001/07/15/IN1593682.DTL&hw=admit&sn=169&sc=507.

Swain, Carol M.. "Do Blacks Deserve a National Apology? Should Today's Citizenry Be Held Morally and Financially Accountable for the Misdeeds of America's Forefathers?" *USA Today*. 132.2704 (January 2004): 30–31.

Taylor, Stuart. "Do African-Americans Really Want Racial Preferences?" *National Journal*. December 20, 2002. http://www.cir-usa.org/articles/182.html.

Willert, Sheryl J. "Affirmative Action: The Benefits of Diversity." *National Law Journal*. (September 8, 2003): 31.

Bibliography of Books

Constructing a Life Philosophy

Angeles, Peter, ed. *Critiques of God*. New York: Prometheus, 1976.

Berman, Phillip L. ed. *The Courage of Conviction*. New York: Ballantine, 1986.

Bhaskarananda, Swami. *The Essentials of Hinduism: A Comprehensive Overview of the World's Oldest Religion*. Seattle, WA: Viveka Press, 2002.

Brussat, Frederic and Mary Ann Brussat. *Spiritual Literacy: Reading the Sacred in Everyday Life*. New York: Scribner, 1996.

Dawkins, Richard. *The God Delusion*. New York: First Mariner Books, 2008.

Dosick, Wayne D. *Living Judaism: The Complete Guide to Jewish Belief, Tradition, and Practice*. San Francisco: HarperSanFrancisco, 1998.

Eisler, Riane. *The Chalice and the Blade*. New York: Harper & Row, 1987.

Fadiman, Clifton, ed. *Living Philosophies*. New York: Doubleday, 1990.

Frager, Robert. *The Wisdom of Islam: A Practical Guide to the Wisdom of Islamic Belief*. Hauppauge, NY: Barron's Educational Series, 2002.

George, Bob. *Classic Christianity*. Eugene, OR: Harvest House, 1989.

Gould, Stephen J. *Rocks of Ages: Science and Religion in the Fullness of Life*. New York: Ballantine, 2002.

Hanh, Thich Nhat. *The Heart of the Buddha's Teaching*. New York: Broadway Books, 1999.

Hunt, Arnold D., Robert B. Crotty, and Marie T. Crotty, eds. *Ethics of World Religions*. San Diego: Greenhaven, 1991.

Johnston, William. *"Arise, My Love . . .": Mysticism for a New Era*. Maryknoll, NY: Orbis Books, 2000.

Kurtz, Paul. *Eupraxophy: Living Without Religion*. New York: Prometheus Books, 1989.

Lamont, Corliss. *The Philosophy of Humanism*. New York: Continuum, 1990.

Lerner, Michael. *Spirit Matters: Global Healing and the Wisdom of the Soul*. Charlottesville, VA: Hampton Roads, 2000.

Mills, David. *Atheist Universe: Why God Didn't Have a Thing to Do with It*. Philadelphia: Xlibris, 2004.

Monroe, Kristen Renwick. *The Heart of Altruism*. Princeton, NJ: Princeton University Press, 1998.

O'Murchu, Diarmuid. *Quantum Theology: Spiritual Implications of the New Physics*. New York: Crossroads, 1997.

Phillips, J.B. *Your God Is Too Small*. New York: Macmillan, 1961.

Rand, Ayn. *The Virtue of Selfishness: A New Concept of Egoism*. New York: Signet, 1961.

Sagan, Carl. *The Demon-Haunted World: Science as a Candle in the Dark*. New York: Random House, 1995.

Spong, John Shelby. *A New Christianity for a New World: Why Traditional Faith Is Dying and How a New Faith Is Being Born*. San Francisco: HarperSanFrancisco, 2002.

Wilber, Ken. *A Theory of Everything*. Boston: Shambhala, 2000.

Wolfe, Alan. *Moral Freedom: The Search for Virtue in a World of Choice*. New York: Free Press, 2002.

Civil Liberties

Bernstein, David E. *You Can't Say That*. Washington, DC: Cato Institute, 2003.

Brown, Cynthia. *Lost Liberties: Ashcroft and the Assault on Personal Freedom*. New York: New Press, 2003.

Chesbro, Michael. *Privacy Handbook: Proven Countermeasures for Combating Threats to Privacy, Security, and Personal Freedom*. Boulder, CO: Paladin, 2002.

Cole, David and James X. Dempsey. *Terrorism and the New Constitution: Sacrificing Civil Liberties in the Name of National Security*. Tallahassee, FL: First Amendment Foundation, 2002.

Craycraft, Kenneth R. *American Myth of Religious Freedom*. Dallas: Spence, 2003.

Delgado, Richard and Jean Stefancic. *Must We Defend Nazis? Hate Speech, Pornography, and the New First Amendment*. New York: New York University Press, 1996.

Dershowitz, Alan. *Shouting Fire: Civil Liberties in a Turbulent Age*. New York: Little, Brown, 2002.

Dionne, E.J. and Ming Hsu Chen. *Sacred Places, Civil Purposes: Should Government Help Faith-Based Charity?* Washington, DC: Brookings Institution, 2001.

Dreisbach, Daniel L. *Thomas Jefferson and the Wall of Separation Between Church and State*. New York: New York University Press, 2003.

Eaton, Joseph W. *The Privacy Card: A Low Cost Strategy to Combat Terrorism*. Lanham, MD: Rowman & Littlefield, 2003.

Fisher, Louis. *Religious Liberty in America: Political Safeguards*. Lawrence: University of Kansas Press, 2002.

French, David. *A Season for Justice: Defending the Rights of the Christian Home, Church, and School*. Nashville: Broadman & Holman, 2002.

Garfinkel, Simson. *Database Nation: The Death of Privacy in the 21st Century*. Sebastopol, CA: O'Reilly, 2000.

Goldberg, Danny, Robert Greenwald, and Victor Goldberg. *It's a Free Country: Personal Freedom in America After September 11*. Brooklyn, NY: Akashic, 2002.

Hamburger, Philip. *Separation of Church and State*. Boston: Harvard University Press, 2002.

Harer, John B. and Eugenia E. Harrell. *People For and Against Unrestricted Expression*. Westport, CT: Greenwood, 2002.

Hensley, Thomas R. *The Boundaries of Freedom of Expression & Order in American Democracy*. Kent, OH: Kent State University Press, 2001.

Hyatt, Michael S. *Invasion of Privacy: How to Protect Yourself in the Digital Age*. Washington, DC: Regnery, 2001.

Jenkins, Philip. *Beyond Tolerance: Child Pornography on the Internet*. New York: New York University Press, 2003.

Kaminer, Wendy. *Free for All: Defending Liberty in America Today*. Boston: Beacon, 2002.

Konvitz, Milton Ridvas. *Fundamental Liberties of a Free People: Religion, Speech, Press, Assembly*. Somerset, NJ: Transaction, 2003.

Levinson, Nan. *Outspoken: Free Speech Stories*. Berkeley: University of California Press, 2003.

Lyon, David. *Surveillance as Social Sorting: Privacy, Risk, and Automated Discrimination*. New York: Routledge, 2002.

Magee, James. *Freedom of Expression.* Westport, CT: Greenwood, 2002.

Matas, David. *Bloody Words: Hate and Free Speech.* Winnipeg, Canada: Blizzard, 2001.

Michaels, C. William and Wei-Bin Zhang. *No Greater Threat: America After September 11 and the Rise of a National Security State.* New York: Algora, 2002.

Miller, William Lee. *The First Liberty: America's Foundation in Religious Freedom.* Washington, DC: Georgetown University Press, 2003.

Owen, J. Judd. *Religion and the Demise of Liberal Rationalism: The Foundational Crisis of the Separation of Church and State.* Chicago: University of Chicago Press, 2001.

Passavant, Paul. *No Escape: Freedom of Speech and the Paradox of Rights.* New York: New York University Press, 2002.

Richards, David A.J. *Free Speech and the Politics of Identity.* New York: Oxford University Press, 2000.

Sadurski, Wojciech. *Freedom of Speech and Its Limits.* New York: Kluwer, 2002.

Smith, Stephen D. *Getting Over Equality: A Critical Diagnosis of Religious Freedom in America.* New York: New York University Press, 2001.

Soley, Lawrence. *Censorship, Inc.: The Corporate Threat to Free Speech in the United States.* New York: Monthly Review, 2002.

Strossen, Nadine. *Defending Pornography: Free Speech, Sex, and the Fight for Women's Rights.* New York: New York University Press, 2000.

Tsesis, Alexander. *Destructive Messages: How Hate Speech Paves the Way for Harmful Social Movements.* New York: New York University Press, 2002.

Van Der Plas, Els, Malu Halasa, and Marlous Willemsen. *Creating Spaces of Freedom: Cultural Action in the Face of Censorship*. New York: I.B. Tauris, 2002.

Welch, Michael. *Flag Burning: Moral Panic and the Criminalization of Protest*. New York: Alde de Gruyler, 2000.

Whitaker, Reginald. *The End of Privacy: How Total Surveillance Is Becoming a Reality*. New York: Oxford University Press, 2000.

Social Justice

Adams, Maurianne, et al., eds. *Readings for Diversity and Social Justice: An Anthology on Racism, Sexism, Anti-Semitism, Heterosexism, Classism, and Ableism*. New York: Routledge, 2000.

Asare, William Kweku. *Slavery Reparations in Perspective*. New Bern, NC: Trafford, 2003.

Beigel, Gerard. *Faith and Social Justice in the Teaching of Pope John Paul II*. New York: Peter Lang, 1997.

Cárdenas, Gilberto, ed. *La Causa: Civil Rights, Social Justice, and the Struggle for Equality in the Midwest*. Houston, TX: Arte Público Press, 2004.

Cavanagh, Matt. *Against Equality of Opportunity*. New York: Clarendon Press, 2002.

Chossudovsky, Michel. *The Globalization of Poverty: Impacts of IMF and World Bank Reforms*. Mapusa, Goa, India: Other India Press, 2001.

Cokorinos, Lee. *The Assault on Diversity: An Organized Challenge to Racial and Gender Justice*. Lanham, MD: Rowman & Littlefield, 2003.

Cornia, Giovanni Andrea, ed. *Inequality, Growth, and Poverty in an Era of Liberalization and Globalization*. New York: Oxford University Press, 2004.

De Greiff, Pablo and Ciaran Cronin, eds. *Global Justice and Transnational Politics: Essays on the Moral and Political Challenges of Globalization.* Cambridge, MA: MIT Press, 2002.

Dowding, Keith, et al., eds. *The Ethics of Stakeholding.* New York: Palgrave Macmillan, 2003.

Feagin, Joe R. *Racist America: Roots, Current Realities, and Future Reparations.* New York: Routledge, 2000.

Frank, Ellen. *The Raw Deal: How Myths and Misinformation About Deficits, Inflation, and Wealth Impoverish America.* Boston: Beacon Press, 2004.

Gilliatt, Stephen. *How the Poor Adapt to Poverty in Capitalism.* Lewiston, NY: Edwin Mellen Press, 2001.

Hayden, Patrick. *John Rawls: Towards a Just World Order.* Cardiff: University of Wales Press, 2002.

Horowitz, David. *Uncivil Wars: The Controversy over Reparations for Slavery.* San Francisco: Encounter Books, 2002.

Jackson, John P. *Social Scientists for Social Justice: Making the Case Against Segregation.* New York: New York University Press, 2001.

Jackson, Timothy P. *The Priority of Love: Christian Charity and Social Justice.* Princeton, NJ: Princeton University Press, 2003.

Kamali, Mohammad Hashim. *Freedom, Equality, and Justice in Islam.* Cambridge: Islamic Texts Society, 2002.

Kimmel, Michael S. *The Gendered Society.* New York: Oxford University Press, 2004.

Kimmel, Michael S. and Amy Aronson, eds. *The Gendered Society Reader.* New York: Oxford University Press, 2004.

King, Mary C., ed. *Squaring Up: Policy Strategies to Raise Women's Incomes in the United States*. Ann Arbor: University of Michigan Press, 2001.

Lake, Christopher. *Equality and Responsibility*. New York: Oxford University Press, 2001.

Macklem, Timothy. *Beyond Comparison: Sex and Discrimination*. New York: Cambridge University Press, 2003.

Narayan, Deepa, ed. *Can Anyone Hear Us?* New York: Oxford University Press, 2000.

Navarro, Vicente, ed. *The Political Economy of Social Inequalities*. Amityville, NY: Baywood, 2000.

Nelson, Robert L. and William P. Bridges. *Legalizing Gender Inequality: Courts, Markets, and Unequal Pay for Women in America*. New York: Cambridge University Press, 1999.

Neumark, David. *Sex Differences in Labor Markets*. New York: Routledge, 2004.

Newman, Otto and Richard de Zoysa. *The Promise of the Third Way: Globalization and Social Justice*. New York: Palgrave, 2001.

Nussbaum, Martha C. *Sex and Social Justice*. New York: Oxford University Press, 1999.

Pincus, Fred L. *Reverse Discrimination: Dismantling the Myth*. Boulder, CO: Lynne Rienner, 2003.

Pogge, Thomas W., ed. *Global Justice*. Malden, MA: Blackwell, 2001.

Robinson, Randall. *The Debt: What America Owes to Blacks*. New York: Dutton, 2000.

Steinberg, Stephen. *Turning Back: The Retreat from Racial Justice in American Thought and Policy*. Boston: Beacon Press, 2001.

Stith, Anthony. *Breaking the Glass Ceiling: Sexism and Racism in Corporate America*. Toronto, Canada: Warwick, 1998.

Tomasson, Richard F. et al. *Affirmative Action: The Pros and Cons of Policy and Practice*. Lanham, MD: Rowman & Littlefield, 2001.

Vandersluis, Sarah Owen and Paris Yeros, eds. *Poverty in World Politics: Whose Global Era?* New York: St. Martin's Press, 2000.

Winbush, Raymond A., ed. *Should America Pay? Slavery and the Raging Debate on Reparations*. New York: Amistad, 2003.

Web Sites

Christianity Christianitytoday.com. This site is sponsored by *Christianity Today* magazine and offers a wide range of links to discussions and ideas presented from a traditional Protestant perspective.

Hinduism Hinduwebsite.com. This site provides comprehensive information on Hinduism and related religions.

Islam Islamworld.net. This site offers an introduction to Islam for non-Muslims, with links to articles on Islamic beliefs and practices.

Judaism Jewfaq.org. This Web site includes "Judaism 101," an online encyclopedia covering Jewish beliefs, people, practices, and customs.

Philosophy Plato.stanford.edu. The Stanford Encyclopedia of Philosophy provides an alphabetized archive with links to detailed articles on philosophical concepts, history, and theories.

Organizations to Contact

The editors have compiled the following list of organizations concerned with the issues debated in this book. The descriptions are derived from materials provided by the organizations. All have publications or information available for interested readers. The list was compiled on the date of publication of the present volume; the information provided here may change. Be aware that many organizations take several weeks or longer to respond to inquiries, so allow as much time as possible.

American Association for Affirmative Action (AAAA)
888 Sixteenth Street NW, Suite 800, Washington, DC   20006
(800) 252-8952 • fax: (202) 355-1399
e-mail: officeadministrator@affirmativeaction.org
Web site: www.affirmativeaction.org

The American Association for Affirmative Action (AAAA) is a group of equal opportunity/affirmative action officers concerned with the implementation of affirmative action in employment and in education nationwide. Information on affirmative action programs can be found on its Web site.

American Atheists
PO Box 158, Cranford, NJ   07016
(908) 276-7300 • fax: (908) 276-7402
Web site: www.americanatheist.org

American Atheists has been pushing for the civil liberties of atheists and the separation of church and government since 1963. The organization was born out of a court case that began in 1959, which challenged prayer recitation in public schools. An online version of *American Atheist*, a quarterly magazine of atheist news and thought, is available on the Web site.

American Civil Liberties Union (ACLU)
125 Broad Street, 18th Floor, New York, NY   10004
Web site: www.aclu.org

The American Civil Liberties Union (ACLU) is a national organization that works to defend Americans' civil rights and liberties as guaranteed by the U.S. Constitution. It works to establish equality before the law, regardless of race, color, sexual orientation, or national origin. The ACLU publishes and distributes policy statements, pamphlets, and the semi-annual newsletter *Civil Liberties Alert.*

American Friends Service Committee (AFSC)
1501 Cherry Street, Philadelphia, PA   19102
(215) 241-7000 • fax: (215) 241-7275
e-mail: afscinfo@afsc.org
Web site: www.afsc.org

The American Friends Service Committee (AFSC) is a Quaker organization that attempts to relieve human suffering and find new approaches to world peace and social justice through nonviolence. Its publications include the periodical *Quaker Action* and the newsletter *Toward Peace and Justice.* It has also published *Human Rights Report: Voices from the Border,* which is available on its Web site.

American Humanist Association
1777 T Street NW, Washington, DC   20009-7125
(800) 837-3792 • fax: (202) 238-9003
Web site: www.americanhumanist.org

The American Humanist Association strives to bring about a progressive society where being "good without God" is an accepted way of life. They accomplish this through the defense of civil liberties and secular governance, outreach to the growing number of people without religious belief or preference, and a continued refinement and advancement of the humanist worldview. The association publishes *Humanist* magazine, and the Web site provides a forum for ideas from a humanist perspective.

Americans United for Separation of Church and State (AUSCS)

518 C Street NE, Washington, DC 20002
(202) 466-3234 • fax: (202) 466-2587
e-mail: americansunited@au.org
Web site: www.au.org

Americans United for Separation of Church and State (AUSCS) works to protect religious freedom for all Americans. Its principal means of action are litigation, education, and advocacy. It opposes the passing of either federal or state laws that threaten the separation of church and state. Its publications include brochures, pamphlets, and the monthly newsletter *Church and State.*

Cato Institute

1000 Massachusetts Avenue NW
Washington, DC 20001-5403
(202) 842-0200 • fax: (202) 842-3490
Web site: www.cato.org

The Cato Institute is a libertarian public policy research foundation dedicated to limiting the control of government and protecting individual liberties. It offers numerous publications on public policy issues, including the triannual *Cato Journal,* the bimonthly newsletter *Cato Policy Report,* and the quarterly magazine *Regulation.*

Center of Concern

1225 Otis Street NE, Washington, DC 20017
(202) 635-2757 • fax: (202) 832-9494
e-mail: coc@coc.org
Web site: www.coc.org

The Center of Concern engages in social analysis, theological reflection, policy advocacy, and public education on issues of justice and peace. Its programs and writings include subjects such as international development, women's roles, economic alternatives, and a theology based on justice for all peoples. It publishes the bimonthly newsletter *Center Focus* and numerous papers and books, including *Opting for the Poor: A Challenge for North Americans.*

Center for Democracy & Technology (CDT)
1634 I Street NW, Suite 1100, Washington, DC   20006
(202) 637-9800 • fax: (202) 637-0968
Web site: www.cdt.org

The mission of the Center for Democracy & Technology (CDT) is to develop public policy solutions that advance constitutional civil liberties and democratic values in new computer and communications media. Its publications include issue briefs, policy papers, and *CDT Policy Posts*, an online publication that covers issues regarding the civil liberties of people using the information highway.

Center for Economic and Social Justice
PO Box 40711, Washington, DC   20016
(703) 243-5155 • fax: (703) 243-5935
e-mail: thirdway@cesj.org
Web site: www.cesj.org

The Center for Economic and Social Justice is a nonprofit, nonpartisan, ecumenical, all-volunteer organization. It promotes a free enterprise approach to global economic justice through expanded capital ownership. Among its publications are *Toward Economic and Social Justice* and *The Capitalist Manifesto*. Press releases and other materials are available on its Web site.

Center for Equal Opportunity (CEO)
7700 Leesburg Pike, Suite 231, Falls Church, VA   22043
(703) 442-0066 • fax: (703) 442-0449
Web site: www.ceousa.org

The Center for Equal Opportunity (CEO) is a think tank devoted exclusively to the promotion of color-blind equal opportunity and racial harmony. CEO sponsors conferences, supports research, and publishes policy briefs on issues related to race, ethnicity, assimilation, and public policy. *The Tragedy of Civil Rights: How Equal Opportunity Became Equal Results* and *Not a Close Question: Preferences in University Admissions* are among its publications.

The Center for Progressive Christianity (TCPC)
4916 Point Fosdick Drive NW, Suite 148
Gig Harbor, WA   98335
(253) 303-0022
Web site: www.tcpc.org

The Center for Progressive Christianity (TCPC) works to give a strong voice to progressive Christianity churches and those who advocate of progressive Christianity. The center reaches out to those whom organized religion has proved ineffectual, irrelevant, or repressive, and those who have given up on or are unacquainted with it. Through its Web site, the center offers resources for progressive churches, organizations, individuals, and others with connections to Christianity.

Claremont Institute
937 West Foothill Boulevard, Suite E, Claremont, CA   91711
(909) 621-6825 • fax: (909) 626-8724
e-mail: info@claremont.org
Web site: www.claremont.org

The Claremont Institute aims to restore the principles of the American founding in social policies. It supports limited government and opposes affirmative action initiatives. Its publications include *America's Passion for Fairness* and *Equal Opportunity Denied: Nine Case Studies in Reverse Discrimination.*

David Horowitz Freedom Center
PO Box 55089, Sherman Oaks, CA   91499-1964
Web site: www.horowitzfreedomcenter.org

The David Horowitz Freedom Center, formerly the Center for the Study of Popular Culture, works to defend America's free society through educating the public to preserve traditional constitutional values. The center's ongoing programs work on many fronts to preserve intellectual diversity and to counter political correctness and a leftist monopoly in schools and the media. *FrontPage Magazine* is the center's online magazine.

Economic Policy Institute

1333 H Street NW, Suite 300, East Tower
Washington, DC   20005-4707
(202) 775-8810 • fax: (202) 775-0819
e-mail: epi@epi.org
Web site: www.epi.org

The Economic Policy Institute conducts research and promotes education programs on economic policy issues, particularly the economics of poverty, unemployment, and American industry. It supports organized labor and living wage ordinances. It publishes the triannual *Economic Policy Institute Journal*.

Global Exchange

2017 Mission Street, 2nd Floor, San Francisco, CA   94110
(415) 255-7296 • fax: (415) 255-7498
Web site: www.globalexchange.org

Global Exchange is a nonprofit organization that promotes social justice, environmental sustainability, and grassroots activism on international human rights issues. Global Exchange produces various books, videos, and other educational programs and materials concerning human rights.

The Heritage Foundation

214 Massachusetts Avenue NE, Washington, DC   20002-4999
(202) 546-4400 • fax: (202) 546-8328
e-mail: info@heritage.org
Web site: www.heritage.org

The Heritage Foundation is a conservative public policy organization dedicated to free-market principles, individual liberty, and limited government. It favors limiting freedom of the press when that freedom threatens national security. Its resident scholars publish position papers on a wide range of issues through publications such as the weekly *Backgrounder* and the quarterly *Policy Review*.

Human Rights Watch

350 Fifth Avenue, 34th Floor, New York, NY   10118-3299
(212) 290-4700 • fax: (212) 736-1300
e-mail: hrwnyc@hrw.org
Web site: www.hrw.org

Human Rights Watch regularly investigates human rights abuses in over seventy countries around the world. It promotes civil liberties and defends freedom of thought, due process, and equal protection of the law. Its goal is to hold governments accountable for human rights violations they may commit against individuals because of their political, ethnic, or religious affiliations. It publishes the *Human Rights Watch Quarterly Newsletter*, the annual *Human Rights Watch World Report*, and a semiannual publications catalog.

Independent Women's Forum (IWF)

4400 Jenifer Street, Suite 240, Washington, DC   20015
(202) 419-1820
e-mail: info@iwf.org
Web site: www.iwf.org

The Independent Women's Forum (IWF) is a nonprofit, nonpartisan organization founded by women to foster public education and debate about legal, social, and economic policies affecting women and families. It opposes the women-as-victims, pro-big-government ideology of radical feminism. News releases and commentaries on issues such as the gender wage gap are published on its Web site.

Institute for a Drug-Free Workplace

10701 Parkridge Boulevard, Suite 300, Reston, VA   20191
(703) 391-7222 • fax: (703) 391-7223

e-mail: institute@drugfreeworkplace.org
Web site: www.drugfreeworkplace.org

The Institute for a Drug-Free Workplace is dedicated to preserving the rights of employers and employees who participate in substance abuse prevention programs and to positively influence the national debate on the issue of drug abuse in the workplace. It publishes the *Guide to Dangerous Drugs*, pamphlets *What Every Employee Should Know About Drug Abuse: Answers to 20 Good Questions* and *Does Drug Testing Work?*, and several fact sheets.

Josephson Institute

9841 Airport Boulevard, Suite 300, Los Angeles, CA   90045
(800) 711-2670 • fax: (310) 846-4858
Web site: www.josephsoninstitute.org

The Josephson Institute develops and delivers services and materials to increase ethical commitment, competence, and practice in all segments of society. The nonprofit organization's mission is to improve the ethical quality of society by changing personal and organization decision making and behavior. The Web site provides information on the institute's programs for youth, sports, business, public service, and policing.

The Living Wage Resource Center

739 Eighth Street SE, Washington, DC   20003
(202) 547-2500
Web site: www.livingwagecampaign.org

The Living Wage Resource Center is a project of the Association of Community Organizations for Reform Now (ACORN), the nation's oldest and largest grassroots organization of low-income people. Its Web site includes a brief history of the national living wage movement, background materials such as ordinance summaries and comparisons, and other materials designed to help activists work for laws mandating a living wage. It also produces the *Living Wage Campaign Organizing Manual*.

National Association for the Advancement of Colored People (NAACP)
4805 Mount Hope Drive, Baltimore, MD   21215
(877) NAACP-98
Web site: www.naacp.org

The primary focus of the National Association for the Advancement of Colored People (NAACP) continues to be the protection and enhancement of the civil rights of African Americans and other minorities. The NAACP works at the national, regional, and local levels to secure civil rights through advocacy for supportive legislation and by the implementation of strategic initiatives. The organization publishes *Crisis*, a bimonthly magazine, and provides press releases on its Web site.

National Coalition Against Censorship (NCAC)
275 Seventh Avenue, Suite 1504, New York, NY   10001
(212) 807-6222 • fax: (212) 807-6245
e-mail: ncac@ncac.org
Web site: www.ncac.org

National Coalition Against Censorship (NCAC) is an alliance of organizations committed to defending freedom of thought, inquiry, and expression by engaging in public education and advocacy on national and local levels. It publishes periodic reports and the quarterly *Censorship News*.

National Coalition for the Protection of Children & Families (NCPCF)
800 Compton Road, Suite 9224
Cincinnati, OH   45231-9964
(513) 521-6227
Web site: www.nationalcoalition.org

National Coalition for the Protection of Children & Families (NCPCF) is an organization of business, religious, and civic leaders who work to eliminate pornography. Because it believes a link exists between pornography and violence, NCPCF encourages citizens to support the enforcement of obscenity laws and to close down pornography outlets in their neighborhoods. Publications include the booklets *It's Not Your Fault: The One You Love Uses Porn, Sex Addiction: Too Much of a Good Thing,* and *Warning: What You Risk by Using Porn.*

National Committee on Pay Equity (NCPE)
555 New Jersey Avenue NW, Washington, DC   20001-2029
(703) 920-2010 • fax: (703) 979-6372
e-mail: fairpay@pay-equity.org
Web site: www.pay-equity.org

The National Committee on Pay Equity (NCPE) is a national coalition of labor, women's, and civil rights organizations, and individuals working to achieve pay equity by eliminating sex- and race-based wage discrimination. Its publications include a quarterly newsletter, *Newsnotes,* and numerous books and briefing papers on the issue of pay equity.

National Organization for Women (NOW)
1100 H Street NW, 3rd Floor, Washington, DC   20005
(202) 628-8669 • fax: (202) 785-8576
Web site: www.now.org

The National Organization for Women (NOW) is the largest organization of feminist activists in the United States. NOW's goal is to take action to bring about equality for all women. NOW works to promote affirmative action and eliminate discrimination and harassment in the workplace, schools, and justice system. The organization offers a quarterly publication, the *National NOW Times,* and publishes occasional reports and papers.

People for the American Way (PFAW)
2000 M Street NW, Suite 400, Washington, DC   20036
(202) 467-4999
Web site: www.pfaw.org

People for the American Way (PFAW) works to increase tolerance and respect for America's diverse cultures, religions, and values. It distributes educational materials, leaflets, and brochures, including the reports *A Right Wing and a Prayer: The Religious Right in Your Public Schools* and *Attacks on the Freedom to Learn*.

Philosophy Talk

3361 Twentieth Street, San Francisco, CA   94110-2627
(415) 970-8020-7000
e-mail: comments@philosophytalk.org
Web site: www.philosophytalk.org

Philosophy Talk is a weekly, one-hour radio series that brings philosophic thought to everyday subjects, such as truth, beauty, justice, intelligent design, love, and happiness. The hosts are professors in the philosophy department of Stanford University, and their shows, including "Meaning of Life," and blogs can be accessed on the Web site.

Reason Foundation

3415 South Sepulveda Boulevard, Suite 400
   Los Angeles, CA   90034
(310) 391-2245 • fax: (310) 391-4395
Web site: www.rppi.org

The Reason Foundation is a nonprofit organization that advances a free society by developing, applying, and promoting libertarian principles, including individual liberty, free markets, and the rule of law. It has published critical articles on slavery reparations, affirmative action, and other issues on its Web site and in its monthly magazine, *Reason*.

Religion and Public Education Resource Center (RPERC)

239 Trinity Hall, Chico, CA   95929-0740
(530) 898-4739
e-mail: bgrelle@csuchico.edu
Web site: www.csuchico.edu

The Religion and Public Education Resource Center (RPERC) believes religion should be studied in public schools in ways that do not promote the values or beliefs of one religion over another, but that expose students to such beliefs. It publishes the triannual magazine *Religion and Public Education* and resource materials for teachers and administrators.

Rockford Institute

928 North Main Street, Rockford, IL   61103
(815) 964-5053
Web site: www.rockfordinstitute.org

The Rockford Institute is a conservative research center that studies capitalism, religion, and liberty. It has published numerous articles questioning government and legislative solutions to social problems in its monthly magazine, *Chronicles*, which are available on its Web site.

TransAfrica Forum

1629 K Street NW, Suite 1100, Washington, DC   20006
(202) 223-1960 • fax: (202) 223-1966
e-mail: info@transafricaforum.org
Web site: www.transafricaforum.org

TransAfrica Forum conducts research on U.S. foreign and economic policy and its effect on Africans in Latin America, the Caribbean, and the African continent. It is a leader in the movement to win slavery reparations for Africans from the U.S. government. It posts reports and papers in support of these efforts on its Web site.

The Tricycle Foundation

92 Vandam Street, New York, NY   10013
(212) 645-1143 • fax: (212) 645-1493
e-mail: info@tricycle.com
Web site: www.tricycle.com

The Tricycle Foundation is an educational organization dedicated to making Buddhist views, values, and practices broadly available. *Tricycle: The Buddhist Review* is the first magazine intended to present Buddhist perspectives to a Western readership, and select articles can be accessed on the foundation's Web site.

United for a Fair Economy (UFE)
29 Winter Street, Boston, MA   02108
(617) 423-2148 • fax: (617) 423-0191
e-mail: info@faireconomy.org
Web site: www.faireconomy.org

United for a Fair Economy (UFE) is a nonpartisan, nonprofit organization that believes that concentrated wealth and power undermine the economy, corrupt democracy, deepen the racial divide, and tear communities apart. It produces books and reports, including *I Didn't Do It Alone: Society's Contribution to Individual Wealth and Success* and provides articles and other references on its Web site to help build social movements for greater equality.

United States Conference of Catholic Bishops (USCCB)
3211 Fourth Street NE, Washington, DC   20017
(202) 541-3000
Web site: www.usccb.org

The United States Conference of Catholic Bishops (USCCB) is an organization of the U.S. hierarchy of the Roman Catholic Church that serves to coordinate and promote Catholic activities in the United States and to organize charitable and social welfare work. It issues publications and statements on many social justice issues, including globalization, third world debt relief, hunger, and foreign aid.

The Urban Institute
2100 M Street NW, Washington, DC   20037
(202) 833-7200
Web site: www.urban.org

The Urban Institute investigates social and economic problems confronting the nation and analyzes efforts to solve these problems. In addition, the institute works to improve government decisions and increase citizen awareness about important public choices. It offers a wide variety of resources, including the report *Discrimination in Metropolitan Housing Markets*.

Index